MY STORY
The Memoirs of Eric Prince and Mary Stathers

ERIC PRINCE STATHERS

Stathers & Associates LLC Publishing

First Printing 2016

LIBRARY OF CONGRESS CATALOGING-IN-PUBLICATION DATA

Stathers, Eric Prince, 1907-1986.
My Story, Memoirs of Eric Prince and Mary Stathers / Eric Prince Stathers.
Pages cm.
Includes index of names.
ISBN-13:9780692711668
ISBN-10:069271166X

1. Stathers, Eric Prince, 1907-1986 – Memoirs
2. Railroads – British Columbia and Manitoba, Canada – History
3. British Columbia and Manitoba – History

Text set in Garamond
Designed by Jacob Eric Stathers, Kim Stathers, and Nicola Stathers

Stathers & Associates LLC Publishing, Bellevue, Washington, 98005

Printed in the United States of America

Front Cover: Left Eric Prince Stathers and right Dr. A. L. (Dick) Lazenby playing banjo.

Also by Eric Prince Stathers:

    IN THE DITCH
    Stories of the Pacific Great Eastern Railway 1929-65

ACKNOWLEDGMENTS

The manuscript for *My Story* was written between 1975-86 by Eric Prince Stathers (E.P.S.).

E.P. Stathers' manuscript of *My Story* was published about thirty years after it was written.

- Harold Eric Stathers, son of E.P. S., shared project guidance and original photographs.
- Mary Lou Stathers, daughter-in-law of E.P.S. shared a copy of the manuscript of *My Story*, offered project guidance, and shared copyright from the estate of Jack Kenneth Stathers, son of E.P.S.
- Dr. A.L. (Dick) Lazenby helped inspire to write his story and provided enthusiasm, a tape recorder, tapes, and banjo playing breaks to help E.P.S get the job done.
- Ian, Ross, and John Stathers and Lynn Fletcher, grandchildren, provided copyright from the estate of Jack Kenneth Stathers.
- Kim Stathers, great granddaughter, helped copy-edit the transcription.
- Nicola Stathers, great granddaughter helped copy-edit the transcription.
- David Pettitt, great grandson-in-law edited the final proof of the manuscript.

Throughout the editing and transcription of *My Story*, our intent was to preserve Eric P. and Mary Stathers' voice and storytelling style as much as possible.

Jacob Eric Stathers
Grandson of Eric and Mary Stathers
Editor and Publisher,
September 2016

This book is dedicated to Joan Mary Stathers (Johanna Maria Uhrich)
known to her grandchildren as Nana Mae.

CONTENTS

ACKNOWLEDGEMENTS   3

1. INTRODUCTION   7

2. FAMILY HISTORY   8

3. ENGLAND   26

4. MANITOBA   35

5. BRITISH COLUMBIA   83

6. EPILOGUE   145

   APPENDIX   146

1. INTRODUCTION

Eric Prince Stathers' memoirs were written in two separate manuscripts between 1975-86 but were never published. Eric named his first book *In the Ditch* and wrote about his work with the Pacific Great Eastern Railway during 1929 to 1965 with a particular focus on recovering train derailments. This second volume called *My Story* describes Eric's family life including his personal recollections of his family background, growing up in England, and Manitoba. Eric then went on to describe his working years in British Columbia living in Squamish travelling frequently up and down the rail line from Vancouver to Prince George. This part of his memoirs was completed in March 1977 with help from Dr. A.L. (Dick) Lazenby. Eric describes how *My Story* and *In the Ditch* were written.

"Here it is the first of March 1977. I had my seventieth birthday yesterday. When I first started doing this story, I would sit back in my chair and think back to the early days. Sometimes getting out the old albums and looking at the pictures. Then I would write my thoughts out in long hand then set them down as you have read on the typewriter. Dick Lazenby has brought me up a tape recorder and some tapes and now for the past few weeks I have been going off by myself in the back room and talking in the tape recorder instead of doing all that writing. Well the other night I had spent a lot of time in the back room and covered quite a bit of ground. I heard a noise in the back of me in the kitchen as I had lost all track of time. I said, "Is that you dear, what are you doing?" Mary said in a rather annoyed voice, "I am sick and tired of spending the evening listening to you talk to yourself in that machine so I am going to take me pills and go to bed." I guess that I do sound funny to someone else but once you get thinking back, I lose all track of time and am living the story over again. The laughs and the heartaches! This has developed in to a much greater task than I thought it would be, however, I have had lots of encouragement to continue so I will."

"Some two years have gone by since I put the last lines on the forgoing part of this book. Since that time, with the urging of Dick Lazenby and the desire on my part, with his help I have put together a fifteen-chapter manuscript of my life as a wrecking foreman that was part of my duties in my work with the P.G.E. This is now finished so I now can get back to doing some more on this work. Today is Jan 22 1981."

2. FAMILY HISTORY

In compiling this work, I have to rely on my memory, for what I have been told as a boy, of the various people represented there, except for those that I have known personally. Starting from the Stathers side of the family tree and then Mary's family tree.

Edward Beacock Stathers

My Grandfather was a big man, with a large beard and mustache. I cannot remember my Grandmother, as we did not visit them to my knowledge after I reached the age of remembering. He was what was known in those days, as an ironmonger in the City of Hull, England. Today he would be a hardware merchant, except that he employed a number of men in the workshop behind the store manufacturing pots and pans and various articles of hardware for sale.

I understand that he came from a large family and had many relatives, as the name Stathers is quite common in the City of Hull, England. He was a member of the middle-class, and in a trade that at that time in England's history was known as the backbone of the country. There is a village named Stathern, north of the City of Hull that may be related to the name of our family.

Eric Prince Stathers family tree.

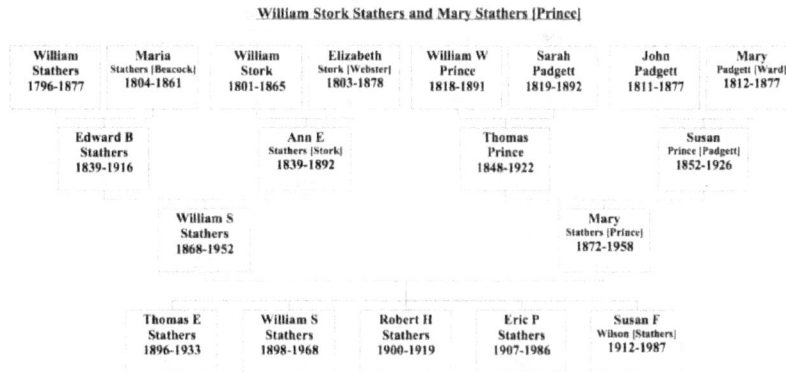

William Stork Stathers and Mary Stathers [Prince]

| William Stathers 1796-1877 | Maria Stathers [Beacock] 1804-1861 | William Stork 1801-1865 | Elizabeth Stork [Webster] 1803-1878 | William W Prince 1818-1891 | Sarah Padgett 1819-1892 | John Padgett 1811-1877 | Mary Padgett [Ward] 1812-1877 |

| Edward B Stathers 1839-1916 | Ann E Stathers [Stork] 1839-1892 | Thomas Prince 1848-1922 | Susan Prince [Padgett] 1852-1926 |

| William S Stathers 1868-1952 | Mary Stathers [Prince] 1872-1958 |

| Thomas E Stathers 1896-1933 | William S Stathers 1898-1968 | Robert H Stathers 1900-1919 | Eric P Stathers 1907-1986 | Susan F Wilson [Stathers] 1912-1987 |

Thomas Prince family tree.

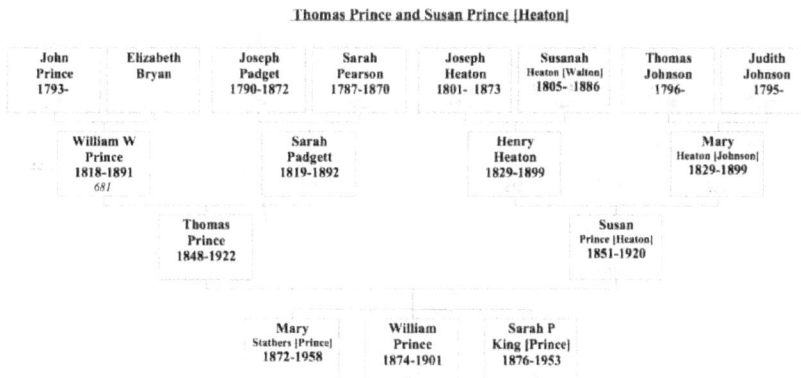

Thomas Prince and Susan Prince [Heaton]

| John Prince 1793- | Elizabeth Bryan | Joseph Padget 1790-1872 | Sarah Pearson 1787-1870 | Joseph Heaton 1801-1873 | Susanah Heaton [Walton] 1805-1886 | Thomas Johnson 1796- | Judith Johnson 1795- |

| William W Prince 1818-1891 *681* | Sarah Padgett 1819-1892 | Henry Heaton 1829-1899 | Mary Heaton [Johnson] 1829-1899 |

| Thomas Prince 1848-1922 | Susan Prince [Heaton] 1851-1920 |

| Mary Stathers [Prince] 1872-1958 | William Prince 1874-1901 | Sarah P King [Prince] 1876-1953 |

Mary Stathers (Johanna Maria Uhrich) family tree.

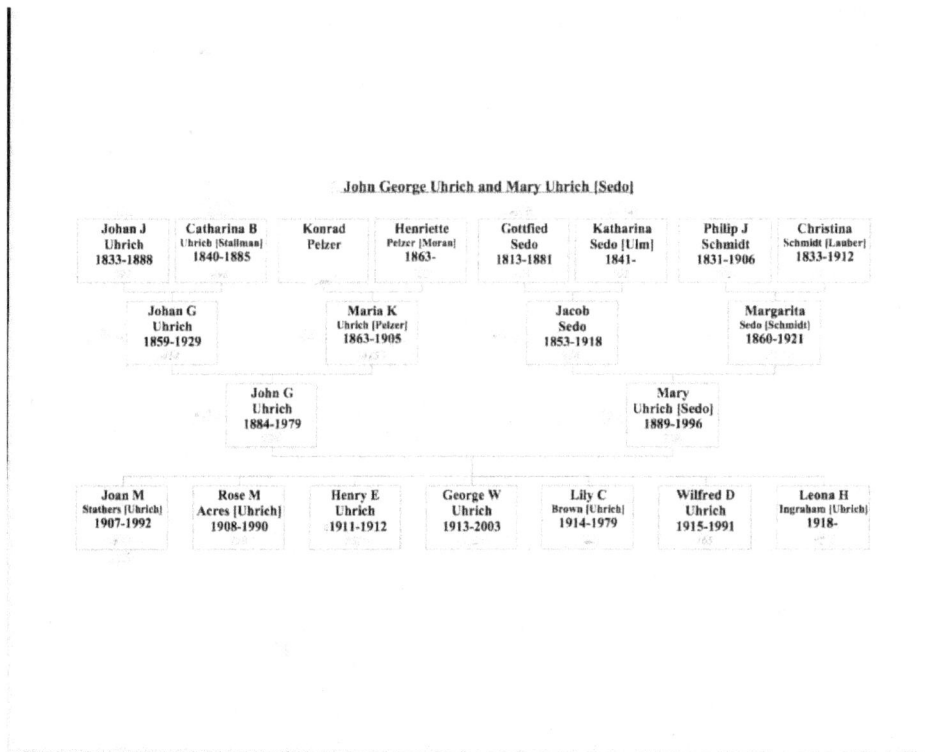

John George Uhrich and Mary Uhrich [Sedo]

Johan J Uhrich 1833-1888	Catharina B Uhrich [Stallman] 1840-1885	Konrad Pelzer	Henriette Pelzer [Moran] 1863-	Gottfied Sedo 1813-1881	Katharina Sedo [Ulm] 1841-	Philip J Schmidt 1831-1906	Christina Schmidt [Lauber] 1833-1912

Johan G Uhrich 1859-1929	Maria K Uhrich [Pelzer] 1863-1905	Jacob Sedo 1853-1918	Margarita Sedo [Schmidt] 1860-1921

John G Uhrich 1884-1979	Mary Uhrich [Sedo] 1889-1996

Joan M Stathers [Uhrich] 1907-1992	Rose M Acres [Uhrich] 1908-1990	Henry E Uhrich 1911-1912	George W Uhrich 1913-2003	Lily C Brown [Uhrich] 1914-1979	Wilfred D Uhrich 1915-1991	Leona H Ingraham [Uhrich] 1918-

Thomas Prince

My mother's father, Tom Prince, was a grocer in the City of Hull. He did a very good business importing and retailing hams and bacon from Denmark. His great hobby was painting in oils, mostly copies of old masters. His paintings were very good and he had many of his best works beautifully framed and some of them have been in the family for a long time. He invested his money in real estate and retired to live off his income. He visited us in Transcona, Manitoba, in about 1922 and died a couple of years after returning to England. He was a short chubby man with a mustache and a short Van Dyke beard that he kept in meticulous condition. He was a devout Wesleyan and Sundays were very strictly observed in his house.

Susan Prince

My grandmother, Susan Prince, was a rather large woman and worked with my grandfather in his store when the girls were old enough to look after themselves. I gathered that she was a great help to him in his life, and was very good to me in our last year in England.

Susan and Thomas Prince

Mary Prince

They had two daughters, Mary, my mother, and Sarah or Sally as she was called, then William the youngest son. My mother was a well-built woman with a regal carriage. I would imagine that she was a very lovely woman in her youth. She had a very calm personality and seldom lost her temper but she could be very determined in other ways. She was given a good musical education, was a good pianist, and had a most beautiful voice. She led the choir of one of the largest churches in Hull at the age of eighteen. The strain of the singing damaged her vocal chords and her voice broke. After that time she could sing for only a very short time then her voice would go into a sort of a croak and she could sing no more. I can well remember turning the pages of music for her as a boy and listening to that rich voice rollout in such volume until I would get all goose bumpy then it would croak and she regretfully would get up from the piano and sit elsewhere.

Her sister Sally was a smaller more vivacious person who married Mr. William King. They later in their life moved to California, then retired first to Victoria, then to White Rock, British Columbia. They are buried in the old Surrey Cemetery, along with my mother and father.

William Stork Stathers and Mary Prince with William King and Sarah Prince.

William Prince

The youngest son William was a most gifted man. He was given a good education and went to an Art School for some time. He made his living painting portraits that were very fashionable at that time. He also wrote, or maybe I should say painted, the official addresses given by mayors and other such dignitaries. It was done in two or three colors in beautiful old English style on a rolled scroll.

Susan Prince with William and Mary.

I have seen envelopes addressed to my father written in this way with little pictures put in the corners depicting the part of the world where the letter was sent. He never married and after he had earned some money he would spend most of his time in one of the pubs. His favorite occupation was drinking brandy and racing maggots. The racing of these fat white grubs was done this way. The owners of the maggots would put up bets that the innkeeper would hold, and then the maggots would be put into the center of the round piano stool in the pub. The first maggot to crawl to the edge of the stool and fall on the floor was the winner and the owner would collect the bets.

My father often told this story about my Uncle Will. He was back in port this time and was with Will in a pub. He watched him win a number of races as his maggots were very lively and started to move as soon as he set them down. So he said to Will, "How is that your maggots seem to get away to a fast start, and you win so many races?" Will replied, "Come over here and I'll show you." So going away from the rest of the players into a corner of the pub he said, "Look, I put the maggot in my mouth between my lower lip and

13

teeth before the race starts, that way they are kept warm and active. Just before the race I turn away and pretend to take the maggot out of the maggot box in my pocket, but instead I take the one out of my mouth with the other hand and as soon as I put him down he is away." This may strike the reader as rather disgusting, however, many things went on at the pubs in those days and I have heard my father tell this story so often and always the same, so I imagine it is true. My Uncle Will died in his thirties of cirrhosis of the liver, a terrible waste of his artistic talents.

William Stork (Sailor Bill) Stathers

Now before I go into the details of my own family, I think I should say something about my father. My father William Stork Stathers was the third child of the family. My father was apprenticed to a butcher at the age of thirteen, but he didn't like the work and had an uncontrollable urge to run away to sea in the sailing ships of that time. He ran away from home and smuggled himself aboard a sailing ship, in the Port of Hull, but before the ship sailed, he was discovered and brought back to his father. His father being a stern disciplinarian beat him with a rod of iron and sent him back to the butcher. All of his spare time was spent down at the docks and one day he repeated the maneuver, but again was caught and sent back home to his father. This time his father saw that he could not stop him so he had him apprenticed to the captain of a ship named the Annesley in the mercantile marine service for a period of five years, which he duly served.

My father was a remarkable man. Five years after he had finished his training he held a Master Mariner's Certificate, which gave him the right to command any merchant ship in the world. Some of his exploits and deeds in his life will come up as we get into the story.

He was an officer in the Merchant Marine at that time. He sailed the seas for twenty years and ended his sailing career in passenger service between Liverpool and Amsterdam in the Wilson Steamship Company. He was five times around Cape Horn in sailing ships and suffered great hardships in these early days of his life. He talked about their hands being cracked and bleeding which wouldn't heal up on account of being continuously in contact with ice cold salt water, their finger nails would be all broken off and bleeding from handling the heavy canvas sails. They were continuously altering the sails as they tacked around the Horn. They were wet and cold most of the time as they bunked and slept in the front part of the ship known as the forecastle. There was no heat in the forecastle except for a small brazier that was used to try and dry their clothes. Only a man with a strong constitution could have stood it for as long as he did. He often said that he whipped his first man with his bare fists at the age of eighteen and I am sure this is true as he was not scared of anything on two legs as I well remember incidents that took place later on in life when I was with him.

He was shipwrecked in the Bay of Biscay, and on another ship and he and the chief officer took command of the ship away from the drunken captain to prevent the ship from going on to the Goodwin Sands. For this they were tried in court for mutiny, but were found not guilty and the captain was reprimanded.

He was ill and recovered from Yellow Fever in the Indies and Cholera in China when the mortality rate for these diseases was 50% and death came to most from those afflicted anywhere from six hours to three days after.

Another story recounted a Lascar Cook aboard the ship who one day ran amuck with a hatchet in his hand. A lascar was a sailor or militiaman from the Indian Subcontinent or other countries east of the Cape of Good Hope, employed on European ships from the 16th to 20th century. My father disarmed him and put him down until he could be held in irons, but in doing so the cook hit him on the head causing a gaping wound which had to be crudely sewed up by the captain. He carried the scar from this wound all his life. He had bones broken and many other things happen to him. Later on in his life in the nineteen twenties after an operation on his stomach the doctor told him that he would last anywhere from six months to a year. However, he spun that story for six months out for about thirty-two years.

William Stork Stathers and Mary Prince Stathers.

After spending years, he came on home one day threw his sea bag on the floor and said, "That's it Mary, I'm through with the sea". At this time he was chief officer of a passenger liner sailing between Liverpool and Amsterdam. He was next in line for promotion to captain and was able to get home quite often. I often asked him why he left the sea when he had such a good job, but he was always rather reticent in his answers and didn't want to talk about it. However putting two and two together from his stories, I think it had something to do with smuggling. Evidently the chief officer of the ship was caught smuggling and my father was a witness. My father had to be witness for the company against this man. As the chief engineer was a good pal, rather than testify he quit the service rather than help to put away his pal.

Smuggling cigars and such goods that were very cheap in Holland back to England was carried out by most of the crews of the passenger boats at that time it seems. My dad admitted to doing it himself as it one of the fringe benefits of the trade.

He then joined the English Army in the Artillery Corps. He was in the army from 1902 to 1905. One day while on maneuvers, he was jolted of the gun limber and run over by the gun carriage. His right ankle was badly crushed which ended his career in the army. He received an honourable discharge and a small pension for this accident but he always walked with a slight limp for the rest of his life.

I think he then went on work on the docks as a stevedore. Then he was caretaker for school. He went on from there to look after a Catholic club called the St. Charles Club. Our living quarters were upstairs over the club. From there he went into a coal business, however this didn't prove to be much of a success. So at that time Canada was being advertised as the land of opportunity and he decided to come to Canada. He and my two eldest brothers came out early in 1913, leaving my mother and the rest of family behind to follow when they had earned passage money for us.

Instead of coming to Vancouver and going into the coastal service on the sea, which he could have done and made a success of his life in Canada, he thought there was a future in farming. He was influenced no doubt by the fact that many people from the 1890s to the early 1900s did very well farming on the three Prairie Provinces. All they had to do, if they had enough capital, was to file on a piece of land, get the horses and machinery, and put in a crop. For the first few years, great crops were taken off the virgin soil and many exploited the soil in this way taking everything off and putting nothing back, until the soil was exhausted. They would then sell out to some gullible newcomer and move on to greener pastures. There were no commercial fertilizers then as we have today.

My father and my two brothers went to a small town in the southern part of Manitoba named Oak Lake. There he went to work for farmer named Wright as a hired man. My two brothers went to work for other farmers in the district. They pooled their money in order to save enough to bring my mother and the rest of the family out to Canada.

Thomas Edward (Tom) Stathers

Now for my father's own family, four boys and one girl. My eldest brother, Thomas Edward, was a dark complexioned smaller man than the rest of us. He was seventeen or thereabouts when he came to Canada with my father. When war was declared in 1914, that fall he and my brother Bill walked sixty miles in subzero weather to the town of Virden, Manitoba to enlist in the army. They were accepted, trained at Camp Borden, and went overseas with the 45th Battalion to England in 1915. In England they were combined with the First Canadian Mounted Rifles and sent to France. He was in the famous gas attack that the German sent over Vimy Ridge where the French ran and the Canadians held the line. He got a slight touch of gas but not enough to take him out of service.

Thomas Edward with father William Stork and brother William Stork Stathers.

Being a small wiry man he was used as a scout. At night he and others would blacken their faces and go out in "no man's land", crawling on their bellies and scouting the enemy lines. At one time he spent eighteen months on the front line and support lines before he got leave to go to England. He was in the war most the time and in action for four years. He must have had a lucky star to last that long.

Early in 1918 he was in an attack where the Canadians and the Germans met in hand to hand fighting. A German soldier shot him in the left arm. Tom went down, the German hit him over the head with his rifle butt, and Tom was knocked unconscious. The German raised his rifle butt to run him through with his bayonet, when one of Tom's comrades saw him and shot the German dead. The German fell alongside of Tom and when he recovered consciousness, he crawled over to the German, went through his pockets and found a beautiful engraved gold watch. He kept that watch as a souvenir all of his life. It was a lovely timepiece.

He was sent back to the hospital in England and while convalescing he married his playmate and boyhood sweetheart, Agnes Early. They came back to Canada in early 1918 to join the rest of us on the farm. Bill was already home. He could not see any future in farming, as he had no patience with animals, so the fall of 1918 he and Bill went to Winnipeg. This was the time of the big strike called by the one big union when practically all of the workmen in the city went out on strike including the milk and bread deliverymen that paralyzed the city. I well remember him going as he packed his revolver. He carried a revolver all of the time when he was a scout and was a very good shot, evidently from much use. He said, "Come on Bill we can't let those Sons of - - - - starve us just after we got through fighting for the country", and away they went. There were a lot of returned men involved in the strike and violence was expected to break out.

This move was partially influenced by the fact that neither he nor Bill could get along with my father. Terrific arguments and bad feelings arose between the two sons and their father. Another factor entered into Bill's case, as I will explain as I get to him. One of the reasons was that my father was a product of the old system, where the sons were looked upon as assets. Most earnings had to go to the family until they were married then they could keep their earnings but were expected to support their parents when they could no longer work. There was no such thing as old-age pensions or welfare in those days, only the workhouse. The father was the head of the clan and made all the decisions for the family. My brothers sent home most of their army pay, which wasn't much as they only, received $1.10 a day. However, it amounted to $20 a month each. My father spent this money as it came in, and there was nothing for the boys to come home to except the farm. True, some of the money was spent on stocking and machinery so who was right or wrong is not for me to say. However, they couldn't take his bossing around since they were now men and had proven that in the war, so they took off for themselves.

After the strike Tom obtained work at the Canadian National Railway shops in Transcona, a small town about seven miles out of Winnipeg at that time. He was employed as a Carmen's Helper on the repair track, and eventually became a Carman mechanic and lived in Transcona for a number of years. Later they moved to Winnipeg. During that time they had three children - Robert, Margret, and Vincent. Another child was stillborn.

I admired Tom very much. He was very much like my father, quick-tempered, afraid of no one, and would tackle anything. He was interested in cars and was always fooling around with old ones, trading them in for others and repairing them. I got along fine with him and there was never a cross word between us. I used to try to get him to tell me about his war experiences, but he didn't like to talk about them very much. Although he did say once that they got used to being shot at, but at times when he was out on scouting parties, when they would be crawling along on the ground or shell holes in the dark, his hand or arm would go through a rotten corpse. This, he said was one of the hardest things to take as they couldn't wash properly to get rid of the stench on himself or his clothes.

During the Dirty Thirties Tom was laid off by the C.N.R. Railway. He tried to get work but was unable to find any as many others found out. So he decided to go back to England.

Mother, Bill, and I chipped in all we could and he sold all of his belongings here to get enough money to pay his fare back to Hull. There he operated a small grocery store until he took sick from some intestinal and liver disease. The doctor told his wife that it could have been caused by poison gas and his war services. He died in 1933, still a young man. However he or his wife never received a pension.

Thomas Edward Stathers and Agnes Early.

His wife Agnes carried on the grocery store and raised the family. The store was bombed to bits during the air raids about 1942. They found other accommodations but of a very poor type. The children by this time were able to earn little money and some how or other was able to live.

Agnes still lives in this place, but Robert and Vince are married with their own families now. Margret married and had three children then died very suddenly. These two men and their families are the English branch of the family and the only Stathers except my own family that have come from the union of my mother and father.

William Stork (Uncle Bill) Stathers

William, or Bill as we called him, was a tall slender man with a dark complexion. As a boy he had some kind of heart trouble but it went away as he grew up. I know little of his or Tom's early life in England so I will start to tell what I know about Bill when he and Tom were in France. They were in the same company together, the only brothers in the outfit. Bill was number one man in charge of a Lewis machine gun, of which they had only two to a company. I've seen in documentaries on TV that the average life of a machine gunner when the battles were on was at most three to four days, as they were the prime targets of the German snipers. Bill lasted about 18 months, and then was invalided home suffering from the effects of the gas and trench feet. He got a larger dose of the gas than Tom did.

There are a couple of stories that I've heard him tell about his war experiences that are worth retelling. As I said before, Tom was a scout. This night he went over the top into No Man's Land. Before he went he told the man at Bill's machine gun where he was going and that he would come in at his gun areas and at about what time. Bill was getting a few winks of sleep down in the dugout at the time Tom went out. When Bill went on duty at his gun the man forgot to tell him that Tom was coming in their area about 4 o'clock in the morning so Bill was on watch when Tom came crawling back to the trench. Bill heard a noise out in No Man's Land in his area and thought it was a German patrol shot off a couple of short bursts with his gun. Luckily for Tom he had just slithered down into shell hole and the bullets went whistling over his back. He was afraid to shout out as it would give his position away to the enemy and he would have most likely gotten a dose of lead from behind. So crouching down the shell hole, he started to whistle softly a tune that he and Bill used to sing when they were kids. Bill caught on and whispered, "Hey is that you Tom". Tom replied with, "Who the bloody hell do you think it is?" and then crawled safely in. Bill said that he nearly collapsed when he found that he had been shooting at his own brother.

Another time the Germans had tunneled under the section that Bill's battalion was holding. Intelligence told them that the Germans were going to blow the Canadian's frontline. The battalion was to hold the line until a certain time, then pull back to the support trenches leaving one machine-gun and crew from each company to hold the Germans if they saw the troop movement. Bill's crew was told to remain behind, so there they sat waiting for the trench to blow and them with it. He said minutes seemed like hours as they sat there waiting for the explosion, but it went off in another section of the line so they came out of it okay.

I well remember the day Bill came home. He was given a hero's welcome, from the little town of Clearwater that was close to our farm. All the town people were out to meet the train when it arrived and the school children were lined up on the platform ready to sing "O Canada" and "The Maple Leaf Forever". I was a big shot. I didn't have to stand in line with the rest of the kids, as it was my brother that was coming home. He sure was a different Bill that came home than that what went away. He had to be helped down the steps of the coach, he walked toward us his face thin and drawn and his body bent over the two canes that he was using to help him walk on account of his feet. I nearly cried and my mother did. Tom was given the same sort of welcome when he came home about a year later.

After Bill's feet got better, he started to work around the farm. One day he was going out to bring a load of hay for the stock, when he saw a jackrabbit behind the barn. So he went back into the house for the shotgun, loaded it and went back out to shoot the rabbit. These rabbits are very good large and good eating. When he got back out, the dog had chased the rabbit away. So we picked up the shotgun by the muzzle and put it on the hayrack. When he put the gun down he must have jolted it as the gun went off, and his hand and wrist were over the muzzle and it blew his wrist away. He was rushed to the hospital at Morden where his hand and wrist were amputated. The Pension Department supplied him with an artificial arm that had a detachable hand and a split hook. This put him under quite a handicap, however he persevered and eventually became quite adept at using his left hand and hook.

As I said before Tom and Bill went into Winnipeg during the big strike. Bill took a course under the Department of Veterans Affairs and became a Sanitary Inspector. There were no openings available when he got finished so he went to work for the C.N.R. as a Police Constable at Transcona. He met and married a Miss Gladys Jones and moved into a house quite close to where we lived.

William Stork Stathers and Gladys Jones.

They had no children but had a very happy life together. She used to work at part-time jobs and they made quite a few trips back to England and the Continent. Gladys had just come out from England before they were married and she had worked in Toronto before coming west. After 40 years of service with the C.N.R. Bill retired. They spent a year in Transcona, a year in England, and then came to White Rock, B.C. and bought a home to end their days in. He died at the age of 71 in White Rock in August 1968 and is buried in the Soldiers Plot in Sunnyside Cemetery in White Rock. The autopsy showed that Bill died of coronary thrombosis. His wife Gladys at the time of this writing was still living in White Rock.

Robert Henry (Bob) Stathers

My other brother, Robert Henry, was next to me about eight years older than I was and had quite a fair complexion. He came out from England with my mother and the rest of the family when we came to Canada in May 1914. He was about 15 years old when we arrived in Oak Lake. He went to work as a hired man for a farmer in the vicinity. After Tom and Bill joined up with the army, we moved to Brandon Manitoba where my father joined the Home Guard guarding German prisoners and internees. Bob, though only 15, enlisted in the army as a drummer in the band. He was a big lad for his age and as he had lied about how old he was. He was accepted. My father thought that he was too young to join up and it left the rest of the family without anyone to help my mother. So dad made some arrangement with the army so that he could get out and Bob could stay in, as that is what Bob wanted to do.

As soon as Bob was 16 he went to the regular Army and put into training. One day they were out on maneuvers and the men had to crawl on their bellies in the wet snow. At the end of the day they were soaked to the skin. That night the company that Bob was in was billeted in an old barn with no heat. It was in the early winter and cold so by the next morning about 50 of the men in the regiment were sick with colds and pneumonia. Bob was among them and was sent to hospital.

He developed what was then known as a leaking valve of the heart and after some months of treatment was sent home to us on the farm. My father bought a little shack that had been built for man who was sick with tuberculosis. It was screened in about half way up the wall all around so my father closed most of it in and put in two windows. Bob and I slept in this building winter and summer for about three years, as it had a small stove in it and was close to the house. For the first year he could not do very much around the farm but as time went on he got stronger and was able to be more of a help to my father. Bob and I got along very well together. We would to out hunting rabbits, grouse, and ducks that were very plentiful around the farm in those days. We made quite a few trips to Glenora together for supplies when dad was away working. He was a good-natured man, had a smile for everyone, and was very well liked in the community. He never lost his temper even with my father who was quite a feat in itself and I thought the world of him.

When the Spanish flu was raging through the country in 1918-19, he took sick with it and that turned into pneumonia. He had very nearly recovered from this when his heart gave out and he died. This was a great shock to all of us as in his last year of life he was living a nearly normal life and was able to work with the rest of us. In that year he had grown to his full height of 6 feet 4 inches and weighed nearly 200 pounds. He is buried in Clearwater Cemetery in Manitoba.

Robert Stathers, age 14 in England.

My sister, Susan Stathers with her second husband Frank Robin.

3. ENGLAND

Kingston-Upon-Hull 1907-1913

It is evening in the working district of Hull, England. A mother is busy doing the evening dishes at the little porcelain sink, before the window that looks out over a motley collection of buildings and houses roofed with slate. The roofs are covered with moss and soot from the coal fires of the city that has filtered down through the fogs that are characteristic of this seaport. Her husband is downstairs looking after the billiard room and bar of the St. Charles Catholic Club, which consists of the lower portion of this rather dismal brick building. The building is two stories high with the caretakers living quarters over the club alongside of a meeting room of fair proportions. The kitchen and living room is one large room in which there is a fireplace with a cheery fire glowing protected by a large wire screen with a brass railing on the top.

St. Charles Club, 81 Charles Street, Hull where we lived upstairs.

On the mantle above the fireplace are a collection of knick-knacks and ornaments, many of oriental origin that her husband, who spent many years at sea, has brought home from his various voyages. Playing on the floor is a small of about three or four years old. Getting bored with the colored blocks he is playing with, he notices a shiny object on the mantle piece. He goes over to the armchair that is alongside of the wire screen. He climbs up on the chair arm and is just able to reach the mantle. However, he cannot reach the object that he wants, so pulling himself up by the mantle he is able to stand on the brass rail of the wire screen. He is enthralled with his position now because he can now look down on the fire that is directly below him. He cannot make up his mind. What is the greatest attraction, the shiny bauble, or the fire?

So there he stands on top of the screen in danger of being partially cremated if he falls. His mother turns away from the sink and see's her son in this dangerous position so without startling the child she creeps up behind him and sweeps up and away out of danger. His bottom is soundly paddled and he is plunked down with a jolt on the side of the sink until the dishes are done and his mother puts him to bed.

Eric Prince Stathers about 1 year of age.

This is my introduction. The very first thing I can remember of my life. I can see that fire in my mind and the fancy ornament on the mantle piece. The year is 1911 and it is wintertime in England. Very little else comes to mind of life at the club except perhaps going with my father to a bakeshop where they sold delicious rabbit pies. I also remember going down to the bookstore and buying comic books for one half penny (that is one cent in Canadian money) and the big Catholic Cathedral at the end of the street with the cobble stone paving. It was there I fell down the stairs, hit my chin as I fell and bit my tongue. I can remember my mother rushing me upstairs and holding me under the water tap and the blood running out of my mouth. I still have the scar on my tongue. All in all I think this was a fairly happy time for our family.

My father then went into the coal business. I guess my two elder brothers worked with him in this venture. Our home again was upstairs, a collection of rooms over the stable that the horses were kept in. There was a central courtyard with the house and stable occupying one side and the coal sheds the other. The courtyard was a good playground except when the horses and wagons were coming and going loading coal. There was an ever-present smell of urine and manure in the living quarters from the stables below. This permeated everything including your clothes; so naturally, the kids on the street called me stinky.

This place must have been on one of the main streets of the city, as one of the most interesting things I remember of the area were the vendors, who daily went along the street hawking, their wares in pushcarts. One would shout, "Peas all ot". He would have green peas, that is dried ones cooking in his cart and you took your bowl out and got it filled with these hot peas. They were cooked with some vinegar added and were very tasty, but the one I liked most of all was the man who sold winkles. These were little sea snails, and for a penny you could get a rolled up paper cone full of winkles. Then with a pin you picked out the snails body out of the shell and ate it. They tasted kind of fishy and salty. Evidently I liked them because I would buy them whenever I could bum a penny from my Dad. Another man sold cockles and mussels that my mother used to buy. She would cook the mussels, shells and all, in a pot of boiling water and many a meal we had of mussels and bread and butter.

It was from this house that I started kindergarten. I can remember my mother taking me to this huge building then going off and leaving me alone with numerous other urchins of the same age. For me the world had come to and end. I immediately set up a terrific howl and the only way the teacher could keep me quiet was to give me a large green toy frog that was kept in a case on the wall. This frog became my friend and helped me over the first few days until I accepted my fate.

I don't know what went wrong with the coal business, but we moved from there to a collection of rooms behind a big building to which the only access was by an alley between the buildings. This was a most dismal place to live as no sunlight could get into the rooms on account of the large buildings all around.

To make matters worse there was an open drain that also served as a sewer across the street from which we were warned, on the pain of a licking, to stay away from and a large cattle feed mill just up the street that imported the locust bean from the continent and along with other grains made feed cakes for cattle. These beans have quite a potent smell and this smell permeated the whole district.

I don't know what my father did for a living in this place, but it was from here that he and my two brothers immigrated to Canada to the town of Oak Lake. There they went to work as hired men for the farmers in the district and my mother, my brother Robert, my sister Susan, and myself were left behind until they could earn enough money to pay for the boat fare for the rest of us to Canada.

Grimsby 1913-1914

It is early May 1913. A big change has come to our lives. We have moved to Grimsby, a city at the mouth of the River Humber on the opposite side of the river from Hull. The four of us are living with my Uncle Will and Aunt Sally, my mother's sister, in their home. Also living in the house are my grand parents Tom Prince and his wife Mary.

It is a lovely home, red brick, two stories, with a large lawn and rose beds in front. There is an ornamental fence with a fancy gate dividing the lawn from the street. This gate I love to swing on, much to the chagrin of my grandfather, who persists in predicting dire things for me to come if I don't stay off the gate. At the back of the house is more garden with more flowers, rose gardens and a small greenhouse where my grandfather fusses over his roses and plants. The back yard is fenced and beyond this are fields that stretch out for a long distance.

The interior of the house contains a scullery or utility room as it is now called, a large combination kitchen and dining room, a large entrance hall with a stairway upstairs. Under the stairs is a large cupboard to which I am banished after being extra bad. To the left of the hall is a large living room with a fireplace and comfortably furnished with large upholstered chairs and tables. Behind this room, which was the focal point for all the day-by-day activities, lies the forbidden ground, the parlor. This room is kept locked up. I guess it was on account of me. It is beautifully furnished with a dark chesterfield and chairs and other pieces of fine furniture. There is a fancy fireplace on one side with a fine dress sword and silver mounted scabbard hanging over it. This room is only used on Sundays, or when special company comes. I must have my best clothes on when I am in this room, then sit like a little gentleman and not scuff my feet on the lovely rug on the floor.

How I hated it! If I could have had the sword and scabbard to play with, it could have been more bearable, but of course every request was denied so there I had to sit. There are French doors opening out to the brick garden. I watch the birds flying into the garden while the adults talk about things that are of no interest to me.

My Grandfather is retired and he spends his time painting pictures, which he is very good at, and gardening. He is a strict Wesleyan and Sundays are rigidly observed. The Sunday routine goes as follows. I am supposed to have worms so before I get up from the table; I have to chew a worm tablet. This is a round little cake about one inch in diameter. It has little colored candies on the outside like on some of those one you get in licorice allsorts. I have this forcibly thrust into my mouth and I start chewing. The chocolate is mixed with the vilest horrible tasting ingredients that the druggist can concoct.

I think that this was supposed to disgust the worms so that they would take the nearest exit, the back door. However knowing that I can't have any breakfast until I have downed this horrible thing, I shove it down my throat with my fingers then stagger to the bathroom and swallow large quantities of water to try and wash out the taste.

This was done under the watchful eye of my grandmother in whose room I slept, to see that I didn't cheat. Then it is down to breakfast. Hurry, Hurry, we mustn't be late for church. Shoes shined. I wore a blue velvet suit with short knee pants and white lace collar with white knee length socks with seams that have straight lines up the back of the legs. Then a straw wide brimmed sailor hat sat on my head, with a long black ribbon around the crown and hung down the side and tickled my ear.

Then off to church all lined up like a row of ducks. The sermon is long and there is nothing interesting left to look at in the church, so after many whispered admonitions from your Grandmother to stop wiggling, it is over.

Now after the pleasantries have been exchanged outside, it is home to a huge dinner of roast beef, Yorkshire pudding with lots of gravy, vegetables, and dessert. After everyone has done full justice to this repast, the dishes are done and it is time for a nap. However, a boy of six doesn't want a nap so what to do. It is Sunday and you can't change your clothes because you have to go to evening service and you must not get your clothes dirty. So I suppose this is the time the cupboard under the stairs usually received a visitor for a while.

Some Sundays the routine varied. If the weather was good, a lunch was packed on Saturday, then immediately after church we went for a walk to Cleethorpes, a summer resort about four miles away on the seashore. This was a high point walking along the country road past cows and horses and then having our picnic on the beach. There were various rides to go on, ponies to ride, and all sorts of amusements for the public. I don't remember my grandfather coming along on these outings. I imagine it was against his religion to do such things on Sunday. But Uncle Will was great fun and let me do most things I wanted. Then it was time to go home. By now I would be pretty tired so I would get a ride on my Uncle's shoulders, then off to bed.

Uncle Will was a fine man and loved to take me out with him and sometimes on a Saturday he would take me out with him on his business trips. He was a shipping agent and had his office in the dock area. I particularly remember one trip that he took me on. He went down to the docks and one of the fishing trawlers was unloading its catch. We watched as they swung the baskets of fish from the hold on to the dock, then they hooked on to a large fish; I think it was a skate. It was huge. When they laid it down on the dock, it took up about half the width of the dock and was about ten feet long. I was a little afraid of this monster, but very interested in what was going on. In a little while a large rowboat came along side of the dock, manned by four sailors at the oars and one man in the stern. We were rowed out to a steamer lying in the harbor and taken aboard and into the Captain's cabin.

The captain was a big man with a black beard, who spoke with a foreign accent. He and my uncle got down to business and I was very interested in the contents of the cabin. There were many strange things in and about that I had never seen before, and no doubt kept private.

After awhile the captain had the steward bring some drinks for my uncle and himself then he asked me what I would like. Not knowing what he had and being taught to be polite, I must have been at a loss to know what to ask for. He said something to the steward in a foreign language and he brought me in a tin that he opened. He put the whole contents into a bowl. It was pineapple, a very rare fruit in those days and only enjoyed by the very rich. I had never tasted any thing so delicious so I sat there and ate the whole lot. Maybe that is why I like pineapple so much now.

School! It was a large stone building with round stone pillars in front of the entrance. One of the teachers or masters, as they were called, stood between two of these pillars after the starting bell had rung with a cane in his hand. All those who were late received one wallop on each on each hand before being allowed to enter this portal of learning. I was always on time, seeing as this reward was in store for me if I was tardy or dawdled on the way to school.

However one morning the inevitable happened. When I got to school there he was with a group of boys in front of him and he was dishing out the punishment. What to do? Keeping on the outside of the group of boys and bending down low I made my way to one the pillars, then slipping around it and behind his back I made my way down the hall and to my room vigorously blowing on my hands and shaking them as if I was just getting over the punishment.

In this school the boys and girls were kept apart, both in the rooms and in the schoolyard. A high brick wall separated the girl's part from the boys. The interior of the classroom consisted of two banks of continuous benches with a raised portion in front to work on. There were aisles at each end and one in the middle of the room. The floor was sloped toward the front of room that had a continuous blackboard on it. In this way the master could keep his eye on all the pupils and the boys had an uninterrupted view of the board. There was no shelf under the desk.

Eric Prince Stathers class picture, Grimsby school, Christmas 1913.

The school operated in this manner. You picked up a slate from a pile on a table near the door then took your place at one of the benches. The questions were either given orally or put on the blackboard. We wrote on our slates our answers. Then the answers were either put on the board or given orally. You then had to see how many you had right or wrong. Those who had some wrong had to put up their hands and those who had them all right didn't. The master walked around the room checking and lord help you if you hadn't put up your hand if you had any wrong. Those unlucky urchins who had to many wrong were marched up to the front of the room and had one wallop administered for each one wrong. They evidently believed in the old adage, "Spare the rod and spoil the child." We were not spoiled.

My best friend at this time was a boy of my own age named John. I can't remember his last name. His father was an Alderman of the city. They lived in a beautiful home surrounded by a high brick wall. The grounds were large on which stood a carriage house and stable. Large trees dotted the grounds and there was a nice man who did the gardening and there were servants in the house. He went to a private school but he lived only about two blocks away. We were very good chums. He had all the toys and things that a boy could wish for, which of course I didn't have. This made no difference to him as he shared all he had with me, and we spent many happy hours playing together.

One day we were playing with some bows and arrows, shooting the arrows up in the air. I pulled the arrow back until the point of the arrow was in the bow. The arrow slipped off the bow, spun around, it struck me just on the outside of my left eye and went in. I let out a yell and the both of us ran for his house with the arrow stuck in my eye socket. We went into the kitchen where a lady took me on her lap and pulled it out. Then she told John to take me home right away. So as he had a big tricycle, I stood on the back of it and he pedaled like mad down the street. There was great consternation when I arrived home with blood running out of my eye. However, my grandmother took over and I was soon lying down with wet cloths on my eye. The scar is still on the left cornea of my eye. I guess I was lucky.

Life continued on like this at Grimsby until it was time to leave for Canada. We were fortunate to have relatives who cared enough to let us live with them as we did. I don't suppose that my mother contributed much to the living expenses as my father and two brothers were saving all the money they could to pay for our passage money. Robert worked as a messenger boy delivering telegrams. He used to wear a uniform with black leather leggings and black boots. These had to be polished every morning before he went to work and I can still see my mother getting after him to hurry up and get them polished so he could have his breakfast and go to work. I guess what he earned was all the money coming in.

Before I leave this part of the story I should mention an interesting custom or procedure that prevailed in England at that time in the middle class homes. I described the house in which we lived in previously. All homes of this class had a large brass lock and a white stone doorsill. On every Saturday this lock and doorknob had to be polished until it shone like a jewel. Then the doorsill had to be cleaned with pumice stone until it was as clean and sterile as an operating table. On a Saturday you could look down the street in the morning and there would be women down on their knees scrubbing away like mad. There must have been some sort of competition to see who would have the best looking front door.

It is early May 1914. The great day has arrived. We are going to Canada. According to the boy's books I have read, this is the land of the prairies, cowboys and Indians, buffalo, covered wagons, and sitting around a campfire at night listening to the wolves howl all around you. Maybe I will have a horse to ride and hunt the buffalo and fight the Indians? There is nothing to fear from them because one Englishman can easily fight a dozen naked savages, that is what the books said when Daring Dick started his big cattle ranch out there.

We go to the train for Liverpool, after saying goodbye to all, which was rather sad. We get on board with a collection of various types of luggage. The train starts up and we seem to ride for many hours past fields, villages, and through cities. Finally we get off the train and we are herded in a long building, there are a lot of people in this building, and they are all lining up to go past a man and some ladies who are dressed in white coats. Finally it is my turn. The man in white takes off my shirt so he can get at my left arm and he takes an instrument and puts some deep scratches in my arm. This hurts but I don't cry. He then rubs some stuff on the scratches and I am sent along to my mother. I must have been the last one of our brood because my mother pushes us all up the gangplank and into our cabin as fast as she can. As soon as we are in there, she makes us all take off our shirts and she sucks away at the vaccination and spits out blood and stuff. She evidently didn't believe in vaccination, as was the case with many people in these days.

The sea voyage was over without any exciting things happening. My mother was seasick most of the time, but we kids romped all over the ship where we were we allowed to go, which wasn't very far as we were immigrants and were traveling steerage.

We arrive at Montreal. The immigrants are kept separate from the rest of the passengers. We are again put into a long building and after we are taken up some stairs and put on a train. I well remember that journey. The car we were in had double seats back to back. They were made of wooden slats and had a let down bunk over each pair of seats. In the bunk were two thin mattresses. The seats pulled out so they could be made into a bed, so the four of us could sleep in one section.

I don't remember any blankets or pillows. Those seats became mighty hard before we got to Winnipeg. All of our food had to be bought at Montreal or along the way at stops. There was small kitchen with a coal cook stove in it, so at least we could get a hot drink. It was sandwiches or what have you all the way, as by the time your turn came at the stove there wasn't any time to cook a hot meal. There would be about sixty passengers in the car.

4. MANITOBA

Pilot Mound 1914 - 1917

We finally arrived at the C. P. R. station on Higgins Avenue and Main Street in Winnipeg. Our belongings were taken off the train and dumped in a pile in the middle of the waiting room. There we had to wait from the time we arrived, late afternoon until the next morning to catch our train to Oak Lake.

My mother made a bed on the top of the pile of luggage for my sister, but we had to make do with trying to sleep on the hard wooden benches in the waiting room. It was a long night, and after a breakfast of what we had left, we boarded the train to Oak Lake,

We were now going through the Manitoba prairies. For about three hours we traveled through a flat country that went off to the horizon on both sides of the train. There were some grain fields, but at that time there were miles of unbroken prairie. We finally arrived at Oak Lake and got off the train, where we were met by my father and Mr. Wright, the man he was working for. There was no covered wagon to ride in as I had expected, the first disappointment. Instead my father put all of our goods into a wagon which he drove and Mr. Wright took us all in a democrat, which was a large buggy with two seats instead of one that a buggy has.

I asked Mr. Wright if we would meet any Indians on the way to the farm. He said I don't think there are any around here. So that was my second disappointment. I then asked if we would see any mosquitoes and he said, "Oh yes. There is one now". He pointed to a large Dragon Fly that was darting about. "Do they bite?" "Oh yes", he said. So I sat there for the rest of the journey slamming madly at these huge insects in case one should land on me and take a large piece out of me.

When we arrived at the farm we were given a house just across the road to live in. It was a large unpainted building of two stories. The house had a large kitchen in it and this was the only room with the exception of the bedrooms that had any furniture in it. There was a stove, a kitchen cabinet and a round dining table, and some kitchen chairs. No sink for washing dishes or built in kitchen cabinets as we have today. There was a large barn that had been blown down in a windstorm. The roof was intact and was lying on the ground on top of the broken timbers of the building. This was a great place to play in for we boys.

I made friends with Billie and Gerald Wright, the farmer's two eldest sons. I thought they looked very funny as all they were wore were a pair of coveralls, a shirt, and a straw hat. They were running around in bare feet, which I thought was terrible. I guess I looked funny to them in my knee-length pantsuit and white collar. It wasn't very long before I was going about dressed as they were. Billie was the one who initiated me in fighting the English way and how the kids fought out here. The first time I took him on after a few scuffles and blows were exchanged I had the good fortune to knock him down. So I stood over him and asked him if he had enough. He said, "Yes", so as it was custom in England to shake your opponents hand after a fight to show there were no ill feelings. I put out my hand for him to shake. Pow! He hit me square on the nose and down I went, then he jumped on top of me and sitting on my tummy punched away as fast as he could. I don't remember just what the outcome was but that was my first introduction in how to you take care of yourself in Canada. It served me in good stead in other schools that I attended.

After we where settled it was time for me to go to school. Came the day, my mother dressed me up in my knee pantsuit with white collar like I used to wear in England and sent me off with the two boys from across the road. The school was a one-room building nestled in a ravine with a small brook running down it about two miles away. One female teacher taught all of the grades from one to eight. I arrived at the school and was immediately surrounded by all the kids who laughed uproariously at my funny clothes. They were of course either dressed in overalls or gingham dresses if they were girls. I was soon put in my place on the seniority list.

The biggest boy at school determined the method of determining your rank in the school. He picked out a boy who he thought could lick you and you had to fight him. You worked your way down through your opponents until you finally found your place. I was down near the bottom seeing as I was only seven and there were boys in the eighth grade fourteen or fifteen years old. I soon persuaded my mother to dress me like the rest of the boys but this didn't help very much as they called me "Green Englishman" so life became very miserable and I dreaded the days I had to spend in school. Another thing that didn't help any was that the teacher put me in a grade that was to high for my ability. The result was that I could not understand the arithmetic that she was giving our class. I made very poor marks and was teased by the rest of the school for being so dumb. This affected my mathematics for the rest of my public school years.

There was no supervised play or sports equipment available during the recess periods and noon hour, so the games that were played became somewhat a survival of the fittest contest. One of the most interesting games played was a refined type of the well-known cops and robbers game that all boys have played at one time or another. The small boys had to be robbers, but not by choice. The big boys were the cops. You were given a head start and you ran as fast as you could, but to of no avail. Two or three of the bigger boys caught you and hauled you off to jail, the basement of the school. There you awaited your trial. The biggest boy was always the Judge.

The policemen held you while you were put on trial then gave the punishment, which was either the Royal Bumps or Beheading. The Royal Bumps went like this. Four of the big boys would get hold of a leg or an arm then swing you up against the basement wall so that your rear end struck the basement wall with jolting thump. After nine or ten of these you were let go and it was the next robbers' turn. Beheading went like this. The furnace burnt four-foot cordwood, so the policemen held you down with your neck and head stretched over a piece of this wood. Another boy took the axe and held it up high over your head, from a signal from the judge he would bring it down with all his might on the wood as close to your neck as he dared. The wood would jump up and hit you in the face and neck and often leave cuts and scratches. This was another reason why I dreaded going to this school.

During the summer my mother and Tom came down with Typhoid fever and were sent to a hospital in Virden, a town about sixteen miles away. Everyone was working away from home including my father. He came home every night as he was working across the road with Mr. Wright but my sister and I must have got into quite a filthy condition as eventually she was taken by one of the neighbors and I by another. The first thing they did for me was to give me a good bath, comb the lice out of my hair, and find me a change of clean clothes. They were very kind to me and kept me with them until mother came home.

War was declared in August 1914. This didn't mean much to me at the time, but in November Tom and Bill walked the sixteen miles through the snow to Virden and enlisted in the Army. They were sent to a camp near Brandon, Manitoba. Sometime after the New Year in 1915, my dad and Bob went in to Brandon and my dad enlisted too. He was put to guarding the German Internees that were held in the town. We followed them as soon as he had found a place for us to live. Then Bob joined the Army too, and as he was only fifteen at the time. He was a drummer in the Army Band. My dad could see that my mother was going to have quite a time with two small children to look after with no man to earn a living at home so he made a deal with the Army. As soon as Bob became sixteen he would go into the regular Army and they would release my dad. This change over took place in March 1915, so my dad was free to look for something else to do.

He heard of a farm for sale in the district of Marringhurst. This is a district in the southern part of Manitoba, near Pilot Mound, which is a large village in that area. Near the village is a large mound about one hundred feet high, composed of earth. The early settlers used it as a landmark as they went across the prairies in wagons, and was quite a puzzle to archeologists as to how it got there, as it rises out of the flat prairie and there are no rock deposits in the surrounding country. He and Mr. Wright went to have a look at the farm and decided to buy it and made arrangements to pay for it on time. It belonged to a widow Mrs. Dempster and hadn't been occupied for years.

This farm or as I will call it the home farm, as we had two farms later on, is located on the bank of the Pembina Valley. This is pretty country, not flat prairie, but gentle rolling and well wooded. The valley is about a mile wide at the bottom with easy sloping sides that were at that time covered with Poplar, Elm, and Oak trees interlaced with wild Choke Cherries, Saskatoon and Cranberry bushes. The fruit of these berries was delicious, not like the same wild fruit of these names that grow in B.C. The Pembina River meandered through the valley and drained Rock Lake. The lake was about three miles up the valley to the west. It was about nine miles long and filled the valley from side to side. It was and still is a summer vacation spot for the people in this part and for the Americans from across the border, seeing as the border is only twenty miles to the south.

The house and barn that were only two small buildings were situated on the top edge of the valley. From the yard we could look south over the valley that was a very pretty picture. To the north lay a stretch of prairie and a neighbor's field, that was stopped by a belt of trees that covered a ravine that ran north east into the valley to the east of the farm. To the north of the trees were some farmland but there was still a lot of prairie that hadn't yet been turned into farmland. There were no fences accept for around the home buildings. People kept their few cattle and milk cows fenced in when it was the growing season then every one let the animals, both horses and cattle, roam at will feeding off the stubble and prairie. Where swamps had been, you could still find the buffalo wallows were the large beasts had rolled around in the mud. In the bush at the edge of these wallows you would find the skulls with the horns still on them where these animals had died. When we were kids we used to play with them, pick one apiece then charge one another with the horns sticking out in front of you.

In May or June 1915 we arrived at Glenora. This is a small settlement consisting of one general store, one school, a post office, six or seven houses and a grain elevator. No station, only a platform to get off on. This metropolis was located about five miles to the northwest of the farm. Mr. Webb, one of our neighbors, met us at the train with a team and wagon. All of our belongings were loaded into the wagon then my dad, my mother and sister, and I found a place on top of the belongings and away we jolted off to the farm.

We arrived at the farm without any trouble and unloaded our stuff on to the ground. Then Mr. Webb went on home. The next thing that took place I will never forget. We all went into the house. My mother was a very calm and resourceful person but what she saw made her weep and she asked my dad if she had to live in a place like this and was this what we had left England for. This is what she saw. The house had only one room. The walls were shiplap that had been papered with old newspapers and magazines to keep the wind

38

out. There was one small window at each end of the house that let very little light into the place. The man who had built it had evidently run out of lumber for the ceiling as he had used peeled poplar poles for the ceiling joists. These were covered with cheesecloth to make a ceiling. The floor was just wide shiplap and was splintered and worn in places. The rats and mice were in the house and had chewed a lot of the paper off the walls and with other material had made nests up on the ceiling so that the cheesecloth hung like bags down between each ceiling joist. The place stunk of rat and mice dung and the place was incredibly filthy, as people had used the house for shelter and garbage was left all over the place.

However, she soon regained her usual calm self then with the help of my dad and myself the cheesecloth came down off the ceiling, all the junk was taken out and burned, then the stove was set up and with lots of hot water and soap and a scrub brush the place began to get clean and by late at night we had a place to keep warm and eat and sleep.

The next day the beds were set up. The double bed in one corner of the room with a curtain around it served as my father and mothers bedroom. They took the lid off a large wooden trunk and put hay in the bottom of it with a blanket over that and it was put over in the other side of the room for me. My sister had a like contraption along side of me so that is how we divided the one room. A large table, some kitchen chairs and a rocking chair for my mother made up the rest of the furniture. Some shelves were put up and boxes set on top of one another for cupboards and we started housekeeping in our first home in Canada.

The next thing was the garden. A piece of the prairie near the house was dug up and planted so that we would have vegetables for the winter. There was a root cellar under the house that had access to by a trapdoor in the middle of floor. This had partially caved in. It was dug out again, all the dirt had to be taken out of the house in pails. Then it was shored up with peeled poles from the bush and shelves and bins put in. Some chickens and a rooster were bought from the neighbors and installed in the barn. They were allowed the run of the place during the daytime, but it had to be enclosed every night on account of the coyotes. Then we had to have transportation to be able to go to school and go to Glenora for supplies so dad bought an old horse called Nigger. He was coal black and just a bag of skin and bones. He never did get fat no matter how good we fed him. An old buggy came along with him so we had that problem solved.

Then came the well. We were getting our water from an old shallow well behind the barn. After the bout with Typhoid fever we didn't want to drink water from a well that close to a barn, so with some help from the neighbors another one was dug in a little ravine just west of the house near the road. This well was about 100 yards away from the house so all our water had to be carried up the ravine and to the house.

When the wild berries became ripe we picked pails of them and they were put down in various forms of preserves and jelly. This was our only supply of fruit for the winter, except apples that came from Ontario in wooden barrels. By the time winter came our cellar was full of vegetables and the fruit so we were all set up for what lay ahead.

As we had no cow we bought our milk and butter from the Webb's who were just across the ravine to the north and about a mile away. Every second day I would go there and get the milk in a half-gallon syrup pail. This I didn't mind at all as it gave me a chance to get away from the chores around the house and play or work with Jim Webb, who was the youngest son of the family. This boy was about five years older than me but he had a great influence on my life, as you will see later on.

My father was very good at curing meats and his hams and bacon were delicious. He could have sold all he could cure if he had built better facilities for doing so. That fall he bought a whole pig and cured it. I can remember the oak barrels that held the salt brine that the meats were soaked in standing in the room. Every so often the brine had to be taken out of the barrels, put in the big wash boiler and pails, and boiled on the stove. The scum was taken off the top of the hot brine and then put back in the barrels for further soaking of the meat. To put it plainly, when the brine was boiling it stunk and the house would smell of it for days, but things like that didn't matter as long as you ate. The hams and bacon after they had soaked long enough were hung up in the rafters to dry. They were also smoked as whenever the top of the heater was lifted off to put wood into the stove the smoke would go up through the ceiling and permeate the meat. This helped to give them their delicious flavor.

Before the winter set in Dad had got enough shiplap to cover the ceiling poles so we had a nice warm place to sleep for my sister and I. At times it was rather smoky but when it thirty or forty below outside you could put up with a little smoke. There was also a removable ladder that you climbed up through the trap door in the ceiling to get to bed. Oh yes, the Thunder Mug. A most important piece of furniture, as once you got up there you stayed as there was no bathroom and it was a long way to the John especially in the winter,

James Webb was the youngest son of our neighbors across the ravine to the north of us. He was a short well-built, wiry and very agile lad about four years older than I. At one time he had an uncle live with them who had been a captain in the British Army. This man had given Jim lessons in boxing and wrestling so he was very good with his fists, and knew many holds and breaks in wrestling and rough and tumble fighting. Any time I could get away from home I would be over there and he would be teaching me how to take care of myself when the time came for me to go to school. I was a very apt pupil as I still had memories of the hell I went through at Oak Lake, I guess I must have done alright in his opinion as by the time the first of September rolled around the news got around to all the kids in the area that there was a real tiger going to start in the new term.

I should mention the other family who lived close to us just across the road on our side of the ravine. Their name was Sanson. There was Bert the eldest son about a year older than I; then Flora about my age; and Henry who went to school with me. I should have said that they all went to school with me. They had four other children of various ages including a baby. Mr. Sanson was a sanctimonious old codger who went to church every Sunday but was so tight that the younger children didn't have the proper clothes to wear in the winter so they had to stay inside except on sunny days then they would run around barefoot in the snow. The three older ones who could work had enough clothes to keep them warm so they could do the chores.

The school I had to go to was again a one-room school where all the grades from one to eight were taught. It was situated about three miles away from us to the northeast. It had a huge wood heater inside, a lean to on the front of it that served as an entrance and a wood shed, and a stable to put the horses in for those kids who drove to school. Came the day that we had to start I hitched up old Nigger to the buggy, picked up the Sanson kids and away we went. Our lunches were packed in half-gallon syrup pails and as thermos bottles were unknown in those days we had water to drink from a well at the school.

Eric with some of his friends dressed up for Sunday or school.

About one one half mile away from the school on the way home lived the Wilson family. They were well-established people with a large farm, a lovely two-story home, large barn and all the modern implements. There were two children going to school from this family. Walter was about a year older than I, and Una, a girl about my own age. They were both nice kids and I liked them very much. Una was a real beauty. She was very dark with an olive complexion. Her parents could well afford it so they kept her always well dressed and she was neat and clean all the time. They had bought her a piano, as she was very musically inclined and even as young as she was at that time she could play very nicely by ear. Even though she was the best dressed girl in school and the most popular; she was always nice to everyone and never put on any superior airs as many kids do at that age.

41

The Wilsons were wonderful people. As winter drew near they told our parents to instruct the Sansons and I that if a blizzard came up when we were at school we were not to try to get home, but we were to go into their place and stay until the storm abated. They would then phone the Sansons and the Webbs and Jim would go over to our place to let my parents know that we were safe at the Wilsons. The Sanson kids and I spent more than one night at the Wilsons. She would put the four of us crossways in a double bed that was such fun. We used to think it was wonderful to be able to stay in such a nice house, eat such good meals, and have sing songs around the piano with the wind howling around outside.

Before I leave the Wilson family I would like to tell about the tragedies that this fine family had to endure. First Mr. Wilson died of cancer about 1916. Walter the same year died of what was then called stoppage of the bowels, a ruptured appendix. Surgery such as it was at that time hadn't advanced to the point were they could recognize the symptoms of appendicitis. He was going to school with me one day and he complained of a stomachache. Four days later he was dead. Mrs. Wilson died of cancer in 1918, leaving Una and her half brother George alone to run the farm. Una, still in her late teens, one day by mistake used some gasoline to get the cook stove going which exploded all over her and she suffered such bad burns that she died.

I think that it was in December of 1915 that Tom and Bill came home on leave before they went overseas. Tom brought us home a small 32-calibre revolver and some ammunition that I will tell about later on. Dad had just bought a .22 single shot rifle which Tom and Bill showed me how to handle and shoot. I was only going on nine at that time, however it came in quite handy during the winter.

After Tom and Bill left, winter came in earnest. After the New Year there was one blizzard after another. The ravine to the north of us that the road to Glenora ran through filled in level with the prairie. The snow drifted over the edge of the valley until there were overhangs of twenty to thirty feet high. The road to the south that ran past our place close to the well was completely covered with these drifts. The well would drift in every other day so Dad built a shelter out of piles to cover the pump and then we had to keep the tunnel dug out to the well so we could get our water.

We were completely snowed in. No one could get to us and we could not get out. The Webb's could get out to Pilot Mound so they would bring our staples in. We had acquired a dog by this time his name was Major, also a sleigh and a set of harness for the dog. It was my job to bring the things back from Webb's with the sleigh. Major was a large black and white collie cross so he could easily pull a sack of flour on the sleigh across the ravine and to our house.

During this time I could not go to school. I spent a lot of time hunting rabbits and partridge, as they were plentiful at that time. Dad made me a pair of a kind of snowshoes out of two apple barrel staves, so I would strap these on and take off in to the bush with the .22

and usually come back with some fresh meat. This helped to stretch out the cured meats so we didn't do too badly in that department. I also spent many an hour with Jim Webb boxing and wrestling in their barn. He was bound to see that his pupil kept in shape for the time we could start school.

After a blizzard, the sky would usually clear and the nights would be clear and cold. Sometimes at night you would hear the yapping of a wolf pack as they were chasing some unfortunate deer along the lower part of the valley. The trees would be cracking with the frost and there would be an eerie stillness over the land. On moonlight nights you could see right across the valley and with all the snow covering the ground it would be bright as day.

It was on a night like this that my Dad went out side to go to the John. When he came in he said "Eric. Put on your clothes, there is someone cutting wood down below". So Dad and I and the dog went down to the flat below the house where there was a good stand of poplar trees. When we got down to the flat there were two men with a team and sleigh and they had just started to cut down some of our trees.

Dad asked them what they were doing and they replied, "What in Hell do you think we are doing, cutting some fire wood". So Dad told them in no uncertain terms that they were on his property and to get to blazes off the place. They dropped their axes and came up to Dad and said, "We have always cut wood here and you are not going to stop us". With that remark one man slipped around behind Dad, threw his arm around Dad's neck, and had him in a strangle hold. The other man stepped in front of Dad and raised his fist. I was scared stiff and the dog began to bark at the men. Now Dad had been through a hard school of knocks when he was at sea, he knew how to take care of himself. Then it happened. It was done so fast that the two of them didn't have a chance. He had heavy boots on. With one he kicked the man who had him from behind in the shin with his heel, then the man let go of him, in the same motion he grabbed the man in front of him by the coat front. He yanked the man towards him and at the same time rammed two of his fingers up his nostrils tearing them away from his face. The man let out a howl with blood pouring out of his nose, then Dad turned quickly on the other fellow who was holding his shin and gave him a right and left to the face knocking him down in the snow.

Dad then went over to the two axes and picked them up and herded the two of them on to their sleigh. They were a sorry looking sight. The one of them with blood pouring over his face and the other fellow still groggy from the beating he had taken. Dad told them if they ever came back they would get a bullet instead of a beating, so they took off. Dad kept their axes and we had no more trouble with people cutting wood on our place. Evidently word got around about this little party and people stayed away. If they wanted wood, which we had lots of it to sell, they came and made a deal with Dad so he made a few dollars in this way when we first went there.

Eric dressed up with his colt.

Came the spring. It was a fast run off. We had the worst flood in the memory of the old timers in the district. Rock Lake seemed to move down and cover the valley from side to side. The people in the valley farms had to move out fast and live with their neighbors up on top. They lost livestock, furniture, etc. But when the water went down everyone pitched in to help out. Houses and barns were cleaned out, furniture repaired and farm machinery taken apart, cleaned and greased to save it from rusting. People were so good at helping their neighbors in those days. It was a carry over from the first pioneers. Many who were still living had come in to the district and lived in sod huts until they could get on their feet. Many of the sod buildings were still standing when we went there, but were used mostly for cattle shelters.

In the early spring of 1918, Robert came home. He had been discharged from the army on account of his heart condition that had been brought on by over-training for a lad of his age. Living space became a problem, so Dad had bought a small building about 7 feet by 8 feet. A man that died of tuberculosis had used the shack. It had screens all abound the walls, so Dad boarded these openings up, put in a window and two bunks and Bob and I used the little place to sleep in from then on. It was quite cozy, especially in the winter when we had the little airtight heater going.

44

Summer came and Dad was away most of the time working for one of the farmers or another. He was trying to get enough money to buy a team and wagon. Bob was away quite a lot too. I think that he was still under doctor's care. Anyway my mother and I and my sister Susan were left alone a lot. When I came home from school there was wood to cut and water to carry and put in the water barrel to last for the day. Mother was busy with the big vegetable garden and chickens.

To the north of us there was a large Indian Reservation called the Swan Lake Reservation. These people belonged to the same tribe that inhabited the Dakotas before the white man came. Once a year the Swan Lake tribe would go on a visit to the Indians in North Dakota. They would travel the road that went past our house for some days. You would see the horse drawn travois with either large packs on them or men would be sitting on them. The women never rode. They usually had packs or babies on their backs. They used the tumpline method of packing with the headband. Sometimes some of the men would come in to our yard and want water or food. Mother would show them were the well was and give them what she could spare. We were always scared of them, as we were alone. This is where the 32-calibre revolver came in to use. When they came in the yard I would load the gun and stand along side of mother being the man of the house. I could shoot all right, but Lord knows what would have happened if they had got rough. They were a pretty docile people by that time so I don't think we were in much danger. The only thing we had to watch out for, were the chickens. They always wanted one of them, which of course they didn't get.

Mother feeding the chickens at the front door of the house.

45

That fall when threshing time came around, Dad was helping the Webb's to harvest. I was allowed to stay away from school and drive a grain team and wagon. I had to drive from the threshing outfit to the home granary, a distance of about three miles. I was too small to harness the horses but big enough to drive them. I drove my first big team when I was nine years old. It was a big thrill for me.

Winter came and went again. Not so severe as the first one but we missed a lot of school. It was too far to go in the cold weather and after one or two blizzards the roads were pretty bad. What did we do during the long winter nights? There were no radios, T. V., or social amenities. I had a mouth organ and seemed to pick up a tune quite easily. Jim Webb had a violin that he played by ear. The two of us would play together and I learned a lot of the folk tunes of the day and also country-dances. Once in a while my mother would get over to Webb's and she would play the piano and sing for them until her voice would crack. One night I was standing at the piano turning over the pages of music when she played them. This was a beautiful rosewood piano all inlaid and had two ornamental brass candleholders on the front of it. I bent over one of the holders looked down inside and for some reason or other I blew down in it. Phew! The inside of the holder was full of cigar ashes that came out of the holder and all over my face and in my eyes. Mother looked away from her playing and there was a little black Sambo looking at her.

There was an old bachelor who lived near us down the valley who used to come visit once in a while. He had been a soldier and all over the British Empire during his career. Dad and he would sit after supper yarning as they called it. I would listen to them for hours. They would talk until three or four o'clock in the morning. Mother would leave them and go to bed. Finally they would run out of wind and the old chap would roll up in a blanket on the floor and go home after breakfast in the morning. This was when I heard the stories of my Dad's life as a sailor and as I have heard him repeat them over and over again, I think they were authentic. I used to play a lot of cards with my Dad. Mostly two-handed games such as euchre and crib.

The big holiday in the area was the first of July. Every one in the area gathered at Rock Lake for a picnic. There were all kinds of races for the kids, with prizes. Then there were the men's contests: tug of war; horseshoe pitching; wrestling; and other contests of strength. This is where Jim Webb used to shine. He was never thrown by a youth his own size and would take on smaller men and quite often win. The food was out of this world. The tables were laden with good things to eat and you were welcome at any table. We kids used to wander around the various tables until we stuffed to the gills. A lot of visiting went on as this would be the only time some families would meet for a year. Then when it got dark it was off for home so stuffed and tired that you would fall asleep on the wagon floor.

In the spring Dad got a light team and a wagon and some farm implements, so there was hay to put up for the horses and land to plow and get ready for feed for the pigs. We grew sugar beets for pig feed. Summer passed and came the time for the harvest again. Men were scarce on account of the war, so any boy that was big enough to drive a team went to work helping with the harvest. There were no combines or gasoline tractors in those days, so each farmer cut his grain with a binder that made it into sheaves. These sheaves were then stood on end into stacks of eight or ten sheaves called stooks. They were then able to stand quite a lot of rain or snow without spoiling. Then the threshing gangs came around and threshed the grain and it was either taken to the elevator in the nearest town or stored in the farmer's granary.

The threshing gangs worked this way. One man would own the outfit and he charged so much per bushel for threshing. The outfit consisted of a steam engine that could move around on its own wheels, a separator to thresh the grain, two wooden water tanks on wheels, and a bunkhouse built an a wagon that would sleep about ten men. About fifteen or twenty farmers would form a group. Each farmer would have one or two men working in the gang depending on the size of his farm. Then the outfit would move from farm to farm until the job was done. The women would help one another out with the cooking for the gang at each farm. The steam engine could pull the separator with the bunkhouse and a water tank behind slowly from place to place. It was quite a sight to see the whole gang on the move with all the teams and machinery.

The outfit would start work at seven in the morning. This meant getting up at five o'clock, feeding the horses, then get your breakfast and be harnessed up and on the field at seven. Some of the men drove hayracks and picked up the stooks from the fields and fed them into the separator. Others drove the grain teams. Usually this was the boy's job, but if you had to shovel the grain out of the wagon into a granary it was back breaking work. Then there was the man who operated the separator, the man who fired the steam engine, and the engineer, who was usually the man who owned the outfit. Backing them up was a man who hauled water for the engine in the two water tanks and a boy who hauled straw from the separator and took it to the engine for the fire man as these engines burnt straw.

The meals the women put up were really something. For breakfast there was porridge with real cream, bacon or ham and eggs with mounds of fried potatoes, all the toast and home preserves you could eat and gallons of coffee and tea. Then about ten o'clock they would bring a lunch out on the field of sandwiches, cake and more coffee and milk. Everything stopped at twelve. The horses were fed and you sat down to a huge hot dinner. Work started at one, then about four o'clock out came the lunch to the field again, the same as in the morning, Work stopped at seven at night then it was in to feed the horses unharness them for the night before we had our supper. This was the big meal of the day. What we had for dinner was only the practice run for supper. I think the women had a sort of a contest going as to who could put the most on the table.

After supper the men would gather in the caboose for a short while. Yarns and stories would be exchanged for a while, then it was off to bed as five o'clock came along too soon. If there wasn't enough room in the caboose for all to sleep, the overflow threw their blankets on the hay in the barn loft and slept there. It could get pretty cold in the barn when you got up in the morning, as the threshing would go on to quite late in the fall sometimes.

In the fall of 1916 my Dad got the job of driving the water wagons. He got me the job of driving the straw wagon. I drove our horses and hayrack and he drove the boss's team. I was too small to harness the team so I would get up with him at five o'clock and feed both teams and he would harness them. The same thing happened at night when we came in. He was paid five dollars a day for the team and I. Half of what I earned he let me keep but I had to buy my clothes out of it. The threshing lasted for about six weeks so I really felt rich. The Eaton's catalog sure got a going over that year.

Again came the winter and no school for about three months. I don't remember how I made out at school in those years, but I can't see how I could have done very well as we only attended about half the school term. Most of the boys on the farms were in the same situation as they had to take the place of the men who were away at war. There was no compulsory law at that time about children having to attend school until a certain age.

The summer and fall of 1917 was a repetition of the year before. I drove the straw wagon again at threshing time. Late in the year we had word that Bill was in the hospital in England and that he would be coming home early in the New Year.

The house taken about 1917 with the new addition put on by Dad with 2 bedrooms.
Note the size of the window in the original house.

Seven miles to the south of us was the town, or should I say, the village of Clearwater. It was on the C.P.R. branch line that served the southern part of the province, west of Winnipeg. At times we used to go there for supplies. This would be a big day in my life. It was usually on a Saturday. We would start out in the morning Dad and I, and sometimes Bob, would go along. We would hitch up the horses to the wagon and bump along the road until we reached the village, just before lunch. Then we would go into the hotel and have a full course dinner for fifty cents each. This was a big deal for me. Then after dinner Dad would go about his business and I would have a ball with the kids in town. Sometimes Dad would get on the wrong end of a bottle and it would be late before we started home. But we always made it okay.

Sometimes he would go into town himself and would come home so drunk that he would be so abusive to my mother and us kids that we would have to hide from him. I spent more than one night sleeping in the barn to get away from him when he would get this way. My mother wasn't scared of him though and would threaten to clobber him if he touched us.

Clearwater - 1918

During one of these trips he made a deal to rent a farm of a half section of land about one and a half miles west of Clearwater. This farm had a three-room house and barns etc. on it. Bob's health had improved so much by this time that he was able to do a fair days work. We moved to this farm in the early spring of 1918 and when Bill came home there were four of us to work the two farms. A crop was put in both places and things began to look up for us.

One Saturday I had been sent in to town to get some thing and on the way home the doctor's car passed me going full out and turned into our yard. I whipped up the horse and hurried home as fast as I could. There was Bill lying on the bed with blood all over him and the bed. The doctor and Dad and Mom were working on him so I got out of the way. What had happened was this. He had just left the barn with the team to get some hay when he saw a jack rabbit in the field close to the house. He went in to the house, got the shotgun and when he got out of the house the rabbit had run away. He lifted the gun up by the muzzle and laid it down on the hayrack and the gun went off. The main portion of the shot blew off his hand at the wrist and other pellets hit him in the chest and neck.

The doctor got the bleeding stopped and he and Dad were putting him in the car to take him to Clearwater to put him and Dad on the train to Morden, fifty miles away, where there was a hospital. The train tracks ran through our place near the house. The doctor was just getting in to his car when we heard the train coming. My mother grabbed a towel and she and Bob and I ran outside towards the tracks waving our arms and pointing to the doctor's car that was now going down the road as fast as it could. They evidently got the message for the train waited at the station until the doctor got there. At the hospital they amputated Bill's right hand and wrist.

After Bill came home he was very depressed. He would sit there and say to himself, "I came through the war in one piece and what good was it?" However, he finally recovered and started to learn to write with his left hand. This left just the three of us to carry on the work on the two places.

We had a very dry summer that year and the crops didn't grow normally. The grain was so short that you could not cut it with a binder, however, in the end we didn't have to cut it at all. Late in the summer we had a plague of grasshoppers and locusts. They were so thick that we had to put bags over the horse's noses when you took them out. The insects ate up what crop there was so we just let it lay. To one who has never experienced one of the insect plagues you could not imagine what is like. I am not exaggerating when I say that some of these locusts would be like a huge grasshopper between three and four inches long. They would be mixed in with the hoppers, that were much more numerous and the whole swarm would eat anything growing in the area they attacked. We mixed Strychnine with sawdust and grain for poison bait but to no avail.

Haying on the farm.

The only source of cash income we had left was the pigs. We marketed them in the fall and with what we were able to earn threshing and selling wood off the home farm we were able to buy the groceries. I drove a grain team that year which paid more than the straw wagon job.

During the time I spent here I didn't lose so much time from school so I began to catch up a little on my schoolwork. That summer holidays Dad got me a few days work with a neighbor. This man had a beautiful team of six dappled grey horses, which he used to show at the local events. He would hitch them up in tandem. That is, three pairs of horses one after the other. They would pull a big three bladed plow which was a big machine for those days. That was what I was doing for him. I would sit on that plow all day with three reins in each hand driving this big outfit, feeling like a real man. It was comparable to a lad driving a big D8 Cat today. But it was too much for me. I could drive all right but when I

50

came to the end of the field, I would have to stop the horses and pull with all I had to get the plows out of the ground with the lifting levers. I guess the man figured I was losing too much time turning around so I didn't last very long at that job.

Came the winter of 1918. One that many people who lived through it I will never forget. Just as winter struck so did the Spanish influenza. Medical people said it was brought over from the battlefields of Europe when the men started to come home from the front. It was very bad in Europe and North America. People were dying like flies with it and every one was very scared. With the flu in our part of the country came a very severe winter. The temperature went down to 60 below some days. When it would warm up it would start to snow and blow, so people didn't get around very much. We all came down with it at the same time. Luckily the woodpile was up against the house near the front door. I can remember my mother standing up against the stove hanging on to a chair as she was so dizzy trying to make some soup for us. One night we were all so bad that Dad crawled on his hands and knees to the woodpile to get wood to keep the fire going.

The flu started with a headache. Then you would run a high temperature and feel so dizzy and weak that you could not stand up. Then would come a copious nosebleed, and after that you would either get better or come down with pneumonia which was the cause of death in most cases.

As we were all down with it there was no one to feed the stock. Most of the pigs froze to death. So did some of the cattle, as all they had for shelter was a haystack in the yard. The horses became so weak that they just lay down in their stalls in the barn, but we managed to save all of them as they were inside. We lost about half of the poultry with frozen legs so by the time we were able to get about we were in pretty poor shape.

Bob contracted pneumonia after the flu. He seemed to get over it but it weakened his heart so much that he was unable to make a come back. So one morning in January 1919 he died. It was so cold and so many people were sick that there was no one to dig graves, so he was taken to the town and put in an empty house along with other people who had died until graves could be dug and funerals could be held. He is buried in the soldier's section of the Clearwater Cemetery.

Agnes and Eric with puppies at Clearwater farm.

In the early spring Tom came home with his wife Agnes. They were married in England after he was discharged from the Army hospital there. He came back to the farm at Clearwater and the living space was very crowded in that small house, what to do for the future? This was the question. Many arguments cropped up between Tom and Bill on one side and Dad on the other. Many times it was over what had he done with the money they had sent home during the years they were away at the war and how little he had to show for it. My father being of the old English variety figured he was the head of the family, could dictate the policy and was entitled to any monies the sons earned until they either came of age or got married. This kind of thinking the two boys or I should say men by now, would not go along with.

The result was that they both left for Winnipeg. Tom found work with the C.N.R. in Transcona Shops as a Carmen's Helper and Bill took a course as a sanitary inspector under the Veterans Act. Bill did very well. He graduated at the top of his class but as there were no jobs to be had in this field he went to work as a Police Constable for the C.N.R. He stayed with this job until he retired.

Dad sold off all the equipment and most of the stock and we moved into a house in the town of Clearwater. We kept a team and wagon and two milk cows, as there was a barn with the house. There, Dad took on the transfer business hauling freight from the station to the various businesses in the town. He was also caretaker of the two-room school, a church, and the curling rink.

Prohibition had come in at this time and the only way you could get liquor was to order it by case lots from the Government Liquor Store in Winnipeg. This had to come in case lots and by train. Now the big event of the day in town was when the train would come in. People didn't have much to do, which included the ladies would gather on the station platform exchanging gossip, seeing who was coming and going and seeing who had ordered what from Eaton's or other places when it was unloaded off the train. Now the men of the elite of the town were stuck for their liquor, so Dad being the man he was made a deal that he would order all the liquor which would come addressed to him and then he would give it out to the men who had bought it. This way the prominent men of the town wouldn't have their names on the crate and they could get their supply without the population knowing it. The price Dad charged for this service was one crock out of each case delivered. People used to look at the case on the platform and say "Tish, Tish that awful Bill Stathers is getting liquor again."

One Saturday evening he didn't come homo for supper. About midnight he came staggering in the house. He was wearing a long winter overcoat that had pockets inside and out. The pockets were loaded with bottles of liquor and he was carrying some as well, My mother got him to bed and he had the DTs, so bad that he was seeing blue monkeys running around on the end of the bed. I was the only one that could knock them off. So there I stood waving my hands over end of the bed pushing off the monkeys he finally fell asleep.

My mother who wouldn't touch liquor of any kind was furious. She gathered all the bottles up and said, "Eric go to the back of the garden and dig a hole by the corner of the fence and bury these bottles so he can't find them." This I did and we went to bed.

The next morning one man who was a pillar of the church came to the door and said "Mrs. Stathers, can I see your husband?" and Mother replied "Certainly not. He is so sick that he can't get out of bed". The man said, "Well 'er ahem. Did he bring some thing home with him that maybe should belong to me"? Mother told him that she didn't know what he was talking about, and not very politely closed the door in his face. Well that was the start of the procession. Next it was the lawyer, then the station agent, then the postmaster, then the livery stable owner, until they had completed the rounds of the men who the liquor really belonged too. The all got the same answer from mother so they figured he must have stashed away some where in the town.

On Monday he had recovered enough to go about his business. As soon as he hit the street he was way laid by this group that wanted their bottles. However he didn't remember a thing about Saturday night and the bottles, so he didn't know where they were. He then came home and lit into mother and wanted to know what happened to the liquor that these men said he had brought home, but she told him that she knew nothing about it. He and the rest of the men searched the town but it was never found.

When we left there to go to Winnipeg, mother had me dig up the bottles and she hid them in the bottom of her personal trunk, which, he would never think of going in too and took them with us. She had this supply of liquor for many years and the morning after he had been on a toot, she would take pity on him and give him a shot for the hair of the dog that bit him out of her own personal stock. He never did try to find it, but I think he suspected her of having the stuff, so he was content to let sleeping dogs lie, as he knew that after one of his bouts with John Barleycorn there was always something for the morning after. That was the only time I ever knew of my Mother not telling the truth.

This episode that am going mention took place before we moved into Clearwater, but I think it is worth the telling. Dad and I went into Pilot Mound. It was during the time of the war when conscription first came into force. If a man was called up he get out of going if he could get another man to go in his place. The prosperous farmers whose sons were called up would get their hired man or some one else to go in their place. The going price for this was $100. Quite a few of the men who were working for farmers took the $100 and went in place of the farmers sons.

Dad had just put the horses in the livery stable and we were tying them up, when two young fellows came in to the barn. They were talking and laughing about the two their fathers had hired go to the war in their places. Dad saw red. As Bob was home sick from war affects, Bill was in hospital in England, and Tom was going through the worst part of the war in France.

He took off out of the stall and stood in front of these two jokers, each of them much bigger than him and started calling them lily-livered "Sons of B's.. " and other such cognomens of which he had a large supply to fall back on. I was scared and stood in the stall peeking around the end of it looking on. The two of them took it for a while, then as he wouldn't shut up and was attracting the people passing by, they started for him. He turned like a flash and ran to the end of the barn where the hay was kept and picked up a three-tanged pitchfork and started after these two chaps. They turned and ran out of the barn with Dad right behind them and whenever he could reach one or another he would ram them in the backside with the pitchfork. He didn't stop until he had ran them clear out of the town. He then came back to the crowd shouted "Are there any more Bastards like those two here? If there are, "Come on". There were no more so he cooled down and we went about our business. As there were no Police in the town he got away with it without getting into trouble.

During the winter and spring of 1919, Dad was often very sick with stomach trouble and couldn't work. So it fell to mother and I to look after the church, the school and the curling rink. So we would have to get up at 6:30 am and go to the school, light the furnace, dust the desks, and I would have to empty the honey cans from the inside toilets. Boy how I hated the job of the honey cans. Then it would be back home for breakfast then off to school and stoke the furnace so the school would be warm for nine o'clock. Then right after supper it was off to the curling rink that had a skating area around it to light the gasoline lamps and look after the ice, while mother looked after the lunch counter. She used to sell sandwiches that she would make at home and take down to the rink. It was a long day from 6:30 am in the morning to 11 o'clock at night when the rink closed.

Then there was the transfer. If Dad was not able to do it we had a man to do it when I was at school, but on Saturdays and in the summer holidays I had to do it myself. Gasoline for the one filling station pump came in drums by train. When I had to handle them I would get one of my chums help me to load and deliver them as they were to heavy for me to handle. I used to pay him five cents a barrel. So this is how we made our living while we lived in this town. It wasn't a very fat one believe me.

In the fall of 1919, during threshing time, Dad got a job with another outfit hauling water again. He got me the job of fireman. I was paid six dollars a day for this job and I sure earned it. It was up at four o-clock and out to the field where the engine was. The first thing was to clean out the flues, which had to be done every day. I was too small to reach the top flues so Dad would go out with me to help out. Then he would go to the barn to look after his horses and I would light the fire in the boiler and get up steam. I would then go in for breakfast. Boy was it cold and dark out there out at time in the morning. Then all day long I would be poking straw in the engine. But I figured I was a big shot, using the injector to keep the boiler full of water and keeping up the steam so the outfit could run.

Eric playing guitar in caboose used by the threshing gangs.

They were long days for a boy of twelve. I was very glad to roll into bed right after supper all tired out. This job didn't last very long as something went wrong with the engine and the man who owned it had to turn the contract over to some one else. Now I don't want to give the impression that life here was all work. We had a lot of fun too. The hills around the town were great for sleigh riding and tobogganing. We made up bob sleighs and had great time on the hills. Then there was skating in the rink and on the creek. This is were I learned to skate. A kindhearted lady gave me a pair of strap on skates that I could put on my boots so away I went. It wasn't too long before I was fairly good. Once a year they had a winter sports day and the prize for the boy's race was a pair of skates and boots. I sure wanted to win them, so as we were looking after the rink I had all the skating time I wanted. But there was one boy who could beat me around the rink no matter how hard I tried. However, came the day of the race there we were all lined up ready to start jammed together in a line waiting for the starting gun. I had my eye on this lad who I knew could beat me but I got far enough away from him in the starting line up so I would be near the rail. The gun went off with a great flurry of feet and elbows going to get away. Then he tripped and fell down. He was up in a flash but this gave me a head start on him so I had the rail and I never looked back just kept on pumping away until the finish line. I just beat him by inches and won the skates. As we couldn't afford to buy skates for me it made them much more valuable in my eyes.

Swimming was wonderful in the summer time. This is where I learned how to swim as the creek was a much better place to swim than in the Pembina River back on the home farm. In the spring, the first thing we did was to clean out the old swimming hole. So we would swim down to the bottom and grab hold of a clump of weeds and throw them out on the bank. We would have contests to see who could stay down under for the longest time. The swimming hole was just out of town at the bottom of a steep hill. We used to play a game of cars when we were coming home from the creek to see who could run all the way up the hill without stopping. If you made it, you said, "I made it in high gear".

One Saturday night we were sitting around the little fire we had made on the bank smoking cigarettes made out of Kinnikinick which is Indian tobacco made from the bark of the red willow and rolled in newspaper. These things were horrible and burnt your tongue until it felt as if it was on fire. However, it was the thing to do so we all did it so as not to be sissies. One boy looked up the creek and said, "Look what is that"? We all stared up the creek in the darkness and there you could see something white with two arms outstretched on the water. We stared at it and one kid said "Holy moses! It's moving". Someone else shouted, "It's a ghost, I'm getting out of here". With that, we all took off in a mad dash up the hill. We all made it in high gear believe me. We got to the top of the hill and looked back on the swimming hole and there was this white figure almost to the point where we had been sitting. We didn't need any urging but took off for town as fast as we could run.

When we got to town we tried to get one of the boys older brothers to get some more men and go back to investigate, but no dice. They thought we were kidding. So on Sunday we all went back there, rather nervously I will admit, to see what we could see. There was nothing in the swimming hole but when we went down below the hole about a hundred yards, there was a raft. In the middle of the raft was a mast with a cross arm on it and nailed to the cross arm was a white sheet. Evidently some farm kids further up the creek had been trying to sail the raft and it had drifted away from the bank and the current had brought it down to the swimming hole. That was the end of the ghost story, but we took a lot of kidding from the men in the town.

Just after the war the production of automobiles really got in to full swing. The Model T Ford Touring was the most popular car. You could buy one for about $780 dollars. Then there were the Chevrolet, McLaughlin, Buick, and the Overland. These four cars where the most seen around the country and the kind that were purchased by the people. They were all touring models, with side curtains that buckled on and had little celluloid windows. The closed-in sedan type had yet to come on the market. There was one man who used to occasionally come in to town driving a vehicle of ancient vintage. It was a one seater Democrat with a platform on the back of the seat like a buckboard. On this platform was a two-cylinder engine that drove the back wheels of the machine with a chain drive. He would come in to town with this thing popping and snorting and rattling along as it had hard rubber tires on it. He wore a dressing gown with a round fancy rope deal over his clothes and on his head was a two-peaked cap of the Sherlock Holmes type. There was no windshield on this contraption and he would sit up there with the steering wheel in his hands as if he were driving the finest car made.

One day down by the bridge at the bottom of the hill it made its last pop and it was hauled into town and left at the blacksmith shop. There the engine and works were removed and it sat for a while. Pretty soon we kids found this thing was a lot of fun. We would push it around town some kids pushing, some kids riding, and every so often it was your turn to steer. This was the high point of our day. As there seemed to be no objection from the men in the town, we started going further away until we were coasting down the hill and over the bridge across the creek. This was real fun, about ten kids crowded on the machine and with this weight aboard it would really be traveling by the time we hit the bridge. As there was no brake on it, there was no way of stopping until you hit the hill on the other side of the bridge. Then the inevitable happened. One night we didn't make the turn on the bridge and ended up with two railings taken out of the bridge with the front end of the thing hanging over the bridge. The kids in front looking down at the water hollered for us to hang on to the back end so they wouldn't tip over so we all got safely off and went back to town to report. That was the end of that. The men got a team and hauled it off the bridge, then took it up to a steep hill and let it go down into the middle of the creek and as far as I know it is there to this day.

In the news of today you see the immense hatreds that are built up between different races of people and you wonder how a thing like this came about and what is the answer to the problem. I don't pretend to have the answer but after living through two wars and being in a family that was affected so much by these wars, I have given it a lot of thought. It seems to me that we are a product of the propaganda that we are fed through the medium of the press. I have seen it turned it off and on to influence the public especially during the last Great War. Let me give you an example of how this affects even the children who listen to their elders talk. After the First World War the Americans made many claims as to how they had gone over to France and won the war. This was seen in the press and in various songs of the day. As our boys were home by this time the feeling ran high against the Yankees, as we called them, and as we were only a short distance from the border they would come over to the Saturday night dances at Rock Lake and spent the weekend there. There were quite a few fights between the younger men at those gatherings with the Americans on one side and the Canadians on the other. This feeling filtered down to we boys and led up to this happening.

It was early one Sunday morning when we saw an American car come into town. The people got out at the gas pump and we saw a young lad of our own age come away from the car with a pail in his hand. He came up to us. There were four or five of us, and asked where he could get a pail of water. We told him to come along with us and we would show him. So we took him to the pump around the corner from the filling station where he would be out of sight of his parents. We said, "You want water eh! Well give you some". So with that we pounced on him, took the pail away from him, and held him down on the pump platform and pumped water all over him until he was soaking wet and nearly drowned. Then we let him go and took off to where his parents couldn't find us. I am not proud of this episode but only mentioned it to show how this feeling can filter down to the very young.

It was here that I saw my first moving picture. A man came around and hired the town hall. We set up a big sheet on the back of the hall and the chairs were set in place with a big aisle down the middle of the hall. We set up his camera in the aisle. I don't know what he used for light but he had to turn the camera with a hand crank. When the reel ran out, the lights were lit and he changed the reel for another. The picture was Charley Chaplin in "Shoulder Arms". It was quite an event in the town.

Transcona – 1919 - 1928

During the summer Dad was very sick and he took off to Winnipeg one day. We didn't hear from him for quite awhile then my mother got a letter from Tom telling her that he was in the hospital and had an operation. As the school was closed and not much to do, mother went to Winnipeg and Susie and I stayed home. After awhile they both came home and Dad told us that we were going to leave Clearwater and live in Transcona if he could get a job in the C.N.R. shops. Presently word came from Tom that there was a job for him, so we sold off the cows and horses and packed up and boarded the train for Winnipeg. I well remember this trip. When I left England there was no electric lighting in houses or in the streets. As we drew near the city I could see thousands of streetlights ahead of us. When we got in to the city proper I couldn't take my eyes off these lights and the huge buildings, as they seemed to me. This started very different way of life to me as I had to change from a country boy to a city boy overnight.

The town of Transcona was developed on account of the large railway shops of the Canadian National Railway built here in 1912 to 1914. They were the largest repair shops west of Montreal. Some three thousand men worked there at the time we arrived. Major repairs were made to the rolling stock and many new cars were built in the car ships. A few steam locomotives were built but not many, as they could not compete with the large plants back east.

The huge steam shop whistle dominated the town with its booming voice and regulated the coming and going of the people. It was quite a sight to see these three thousand men pouring out of the shop gates when the five o'clock whistle blew. A shop train used to run to Winnipeg every morning and night with nineteen or twenty coaches on it to transport the men who lived in the city and worked in the shops. More about these shops will be described later in the story.

Dad had made arrangements to buy a small house at 85 Victoria Avenue. His payments were $25 per month. So we had a place to go to. Our furniture had gone on ahead so when we arrived Tom and Bill had most of it set up. It didn't take us long to set up house and we were established again. I was delighted with the electric lights that consisted of a single globe hanging down from the center of the ceiling on a drop cord. But imagine all you had to do was to push a button on the switch and the light came on. No more coal oil lamps to fill and clean the glass and trim the wicks. My mother to her dying day never could understand how the light got from the switch to the lamp in such a short time. As there were two bedrooms in this house Bill moved in with us as a boarder.

Eric in Transcona with his sister Susan.

I started school right away as it was early September. I was put in grade eight. This was a five-room school with a full basement and was a much more modern building than any I had been in before. As there were about two hundred kids going to this school you didn't have to fight your way in as was the case in the one-room schools in the country. Life was pleasant at this school. Our teacher was a jewel. Her name was Mrs. McGregor. She was an elderly lady and wore pince-nez glasses that she was habitually taking off and on as she addressed the class. She had the knack of imparting the lessons to her students in a way that it made it fun to learn. If we finished our assignments ahead of time, she would tell us stories and have discussion on various subjects such as archeology, science, spiritualism, life in other lands, and such subjects. We used to get through our work as fast as we could so we could have these rewards. I did very well in all subjects with exception of arithmetic, however I made a passing grade and at the end of the term in 1921 I graduated with my elementary school certificate.

In my class was a skinny little blonde girl with pigtails. She was very quiet and never mixed with the boys. When Mrs. McGregor would ask her to stand and read from her book you could hardly hear her speak. Mrs. McGregor would say, "Speak up Mary, I can't hear you from the front of the room". This would bring snickers from the class that would only make the little girl more upset. I didn't know her very well as I was always roaring around with the boys and any way girls were for the birds at that age. I will describe more about this little blonde girl later on.

All over town there was open air skating rinks in the winter that were made by various Dads who would get together and flood a vacant lot for their own kids and their

60

friends to use. In the center of the town was the town rink. This was flooded by the town and kept in shape all winter. There was a small heated shack to get warm in and the rink was fenced in with boards so that hockey games could be played on it. This is where I really learned to skate and play hockey. There was a girl in our class named Dorothy Harding. Dorothy was quite a gal for the boys and she was a expert skater. She was too far up on the social scale in the town for me to be invited to her house as her father was a foreman in the shops and a big shot in the town. However, Dorothy and I used to get together on the rink and as we seemed to coordinate very well on the ice it wasn't long until we were trying out all the fancy skating for couples that was done at that time. As the years went on we became fairly proficient at the art. But I was never invited to her house.

I started playing hockey with the midget team, 16 years and under. We were a real rag tag bunch of kids. We had no protective equipment such as the kids have today. We were still wearing knee pants in those days, so we would get our mothers to put an extra top on our stockings and we would split the Eaton's Catalogue in half and stuff them in our stockings for shin pads. This and a twenty-five cent pair of felt kneepads were all the protection we had. We had no uniforms and for shorts our mothers cut them out of an old pair of pants that had the knees worn out.

Eric in minor hockey uniform in Transcona at age 16.

We played in the Eastern section of the Winnipeg League. The city was divided into four areas: Center; Kildonan; St. Vital; and Elmwood. When I was sixteen we won our division Elmwood. This put us in the playoffs that were held in the big professional arena in

Winnipeg. As we had no uniforms the C.N.R. lent us the uniforms from the defunct C.N.R. Hockey Club to use in the playoffs. We were a proud bunch of kids when we skated out on the ice in the uniforms in that big arena. We were playing against St.Vital in a sudden death game. I played right defense as I shot left handed. Our pride didn't last long. There was a huge boy on the St. Vital team who must have weighed twice as much as I did. He was what is known today as a rushing defenseman. A real Bobby Orr type. When he came down the ice it was like trying to stop a freight train. I bodied him a couple of times and each time I ended up on the ice seeing stars. Our coach pulled me out to the bench and said, "Stop that guy or I will pull you out of the game". So away I went back on and the next time he came down the other defenseman and I tried to sandwich him but it was no good, we both went flying. The coach sent in two more defensemen who didn't do any better. They walked all over us and we lost our chance at the cup. After I was sixteen, I played juvenile hockey for a while but we had no backing in the town and the team folded up after a couple of years. So that ended my hockey-playing career except for pickup games on the local rink on the weekends.

I must go back a little now to the time I left school. When I had passed my entrance exam at the age of fourteen, which was grade eight, my father said to me. "Well son, now you are through school you will have to get a job like the rest of your brothers did". So the next Saturday he took me into Winnipeg and got me a job at the Empire Hotel that was on Main Street next to the C.N.R. Depot. I was a bellboy, but I didn't wear a uniform. The pay was fifteen dollars a month with board and room such as it was. We were allowed to keep any tips that we got which would vary from day to day but seldom exceeded a dollar. I worked from 6 am to 12 am then off until 6 pm until midnight one day then the next day you came on at 12 am and worked until 6 pm. Twelve hours one day and 5 the next day with no days off.

The male employees slept in the basement, which was dark and damp. The female employees slept in dormitory on the top floor. I roomed with an elevator boy about 19 years of age, two men to a room. His main object in life seemed to be how many women he could seduce and how many times he could do it in one night. He described his experiences to me in detail, so I soon became acquainted with the facts of life. He was fired just before I was as he was found sleeping with a woman hotel guest when he was supposed to be running the elevator.

The headman was the Porter. He was dressed in a uniform and met all the trains and supervised the bellhops and elevator men. He and I didn't get along very well. We all ate at a long table in the kitchen. We would get the scraggle end of the meat and the burned and left over vegetables from the day before. He sat at the same table with us, but he ate the best of the steaks and chops the same as the hotel patrons got in the front dining room. This I thought was very unfair as I would watch him dig in to a huge steak with all the trimmings, while we were eating leftovers. Sometimes I would get homesick and pedal the eight or more miles home to Transcona after the 6 pm shift, then I would have to get up early enough the next day to start my shift at 6 am. By the time I had got through the most of the day about eleven at night I would be pretty sleepy and would doze off on the little seat that we had to sit on near the front door. He would catch me and give me Hell. One night he slapped me across the face to wake me up, which didn't improve relations very much.

Another duty that I had to perform at times was when the housekeeper who was on the main floor wanted a message taken up to the female dormitory. So she would send me up with a message for one of the girls. I suppose at that age seeing as I hadn't started to grow tall yet I would be rather cute as I was the youngest bellhop on the staff. When I knocked at the door they would grab me and take me inside the room where all these women were sitting around in various stages of undress. They would plunk me down on one of the women's knees then start to tease and tickle me. I would be blushing like mad and trying to squirm away from them. Finally they would let me go, so it became a sort of a game with them whenever I would have to go up there I would knock on the door then back up far enough so they couldn't reach me. When the door would open I would yell out the message then run like Hell for the stairs. What some men would have given for a job like that eh?

Eric with first pair of dress shoes and pants.

The final blow came one night when a civil engineer checked into the hotel about ten o'clock. He had a transit, cases, boxes, and packsacks, etc. I took him up to his room that was down at the far end of the hall, and then I had to make two trips with the elevator to get all his stuff upstairs. After I had lugged all this stuff to his room I turned to go out and he said, "Boy. Here is a tip for you", and he handed me a nickel, five cents. I looked at it, then quickly popped it back in his hand and said, "Mister, I guess you need this more than I do", and went out of the room. He reported it to the desk so the next morning I was on the carpet with the Porter. I was told to go to to this mans room and apologize. This I wouldn't do, so I was fired. I lasted about two months on my first job after leaving school.

After that I would leave home about seven in the morning and pedal my bike in to the employment office in Winnipeg to look for a job. I did this for about three months, then one day I saw a sign in the window of the Ryan and Devlin Shoe Store on Portage Avenue. Boy wanted. So I went to work as a delivery boy for this store. The store provided a bike and a newspaper carrying bag, so with this bag on my back I delivered shoes all over Winnipeg. I started at nine in the morning and was through at 6 pm at night. Sundays were off, but we worked until 9 at night on Saturdays. The wages were $9 a week that went to my mother. On Saturdays she would give me 35 cents so I could have a hot meal in the evening. In the winter time I couldn't pedal my bike into the city so I had to use the shop train that left a seven in the morning, or if I ran real hard I could make it into the store by catching the eight o-clock train and would only be a few minutes late.

Pedaling a bike in the wintertime around the city wasn't too pleasant a job, but as I had other things to do in the store and the people were nice, I rather enjoyed this work. I was out in the open air most of the time and moving around which was good for me. Why I didn't get run over or injured is amazing. I used to hitch rides on the side of a truck, that is I would grab the side of a truck at an intersection and hang on with one hand and steer with the other. This was great but you had to look out for the police as if they caught you doing this you could be fined. Another job I had to do was to go to the post office every night at 5:30 with the mail. I would dash off on my bike weaving in and out of the traffic and at the traffic lights you could beat the cars across the intersection if you got out in front of them. This way you could get over into the lane that you wanted to be in. The cars didn't have the get away that they have today so as long as you didn't slip you were one length ahead of them before they could get going any speed. This was rather hazardous in the wintertime with snow on the streets, but I always made it. As my wife says, "You must have had an angel on each shoulder".

In the summer of 1922 there was an opening for a messenger boy in the C.N.R. yard office that was about a mile away up the yards east of Transcona. I applied and got the job. So I started my railroad career delivering mail and messages to and from the shops, and telegrams around the town. That winter there was a smallpox epidemic in the town and sometimes I had to deliver telegrams to houses that had the pox and had the quarantine sign on the outside of the house. I was scared when I has to do this so when I came to a house that had one of these signs on it I would knock on the door, then take deep breaths until the door was opened then hold my breath until they had signed for the telegram. I must have looked funny going blue in the face holding my breath so I wouldn't breath any of the germs from the house.

There were quite a few men that worked out of the yard office as car checkers. They had to go all over yard taking the numbers of the cars so the switch lists could be made up. We all used to hitch rides off the switch engines. I got pretty sharp at catching the rear of the engine and jumping on the footboard as it was going by. The engines would never stop for you. One day as I was going from the yard office to the shops I saw a group of men standing around someone on the ground near an engine. This man was one of the car checkers, he had tried to catch the rear end of the engine that had some cars behind it. He had slipped and the cars had run over his right arm near the shoulder. There was blood all over snow and it gave me quite a shock. He recovered but lost his arm. I learned an important lesson by another mans mistake, one that served me all my life that I worked on the railroad as I have jumped on moving trains thousands of times. The lesson is this: make sure that you have a good handhold before your feet leave the ground.

During the winter my father put my name down to serve an apprenticeship in the shops as an electrician. In order to do this you had to write an examination and be interviewed by the apprentice instructor a Mr. Bristol. I took the exam and a couple of days later he called me in to his office and told me that I had failed the arithmetic part of the exam. I was very disappointed, however he was a kindly man and started asking me questions as to my background. I told him all about my life on the farm and the difficulties I had in going to school and having to work during the war during harvest time. He was very kind and understanding, so he gave me an arithmetic book, marked off the pages he wanted me to study, and said, "Go on home, study this book and come back six weeks from today." Believe me my nose was in that book continually for the next six weeks. I went back on the day he had set and wrote again. He made me wait until he had looked over the paper. Then he said, "You have done fine, if you can improve as much in the next five years as the same rate as you have done in the past six weeks, you will make a good mechanic. So I walked out of there a happy boy.

I then had to wait for an opening in the shops. In March 1923 there was an opening for a Carmen apprentice in the car shops. There were no openings for electricians for another ten months or more, so I thought it would be nice to be able to build those shiny coaches that we used to see coming out of the shops from time to time, so I started to work as an apprentice in the Freight Car shop and really at the bottom as I was put to work building and repairing push cars and speeder frames with an old carpenter.

The car shop was a huge building. It was 12 tracks wide and each track held ten cars. The noise was terrific as hundreds of men worked here. Oxyacetylene torches were just coming in to general use so there weren't many in the shop. Electric welding was just in its infancy and the machines were huge and cumbersome compared to those in use now. The welding rod were just bare steel rod as they hadn't discovered how to coat the rods to protect the welds, such as is done now. The welds made in those days were not as strong as a riveted joint so most of the steel work was put together with rivets. We had to split the rusted nuts off the bolts with a hammer and cold chisel and you got a lot of skinned hands and swollen knuckles until you learned how to hit the chisel head every time.

The rivets on the steel parts of the cars were cut off with a huge air gun, called a Rivet Buster. This machine took three men to handle it. One man to hold the rear end where the control handle was situated, one man to hold the front end on the rivet, and one man to hold a sack over the rivet head and hang on to the gun when the rivet was cut off. If you didn't hold a sack over the rivet head it would fly down the shop like a bullet and possibly injure someone. It was exhausting work on this machine and it made a noise like a gun going off with every stroke.

I will not go in detail about the different types of machinery that were used in the shop, but it was one of the most modern railroad shops in Canada at the time. It still is as they have recently spent Millions of dollars modernizing the plant. The shop was divided into two sections. The wooden car repair and steel car repair sections. The wood car section was nine tracks wide and the steel car part three tracks wide, as most of the Freight Cars were made of wood at that time. There was a modern air brake repair room in the wooden portion and various little shops and storerooms along the side. This was only one shop in this huge repair center. There were about three thousand men working in the overall plant.

I spent two years in this shop learning the different skills required to perform the various stages of building and repairing cars. Three of these months were spent in the air brake department, which to me was very interesting. I took quite an interest in this work which was a big help to me in later years as I had the theory pounded into my head by a man who took quite an interest in me and would explain the detail and theory until he made sure I had it.

The next move was into the cabinet shop. I really enjoyed working in this part of the plant. The apprentices were only supposed to spend 9 months in this shop, but the foreman was short handed at the time and as I suppose he was satisfied with the work I was doing so he got permission from the apprentice department to keep me on for another three months. So I was one year in the cabinet shop to me the most enjoyable period of my apprenticeship.

Commercial plywood such as is used to day for so many uses was not available then as it is today. In the cabinet shop we made up the plywood panels, the inside core was made up of layers of a cheap veneer of whitewood, a species of Florida Poplar. The outside veneers were made up of either Mahogany or Walnut veneers very carefully matched as to grain and joined so you couldn't see the joint in the veneers. This work was all done by hand then the sheets of veneer were put in a huge press after they had all been glued together and left there until the glue set. The joints of the veneer sheets were held together with a gauze tape that was impregnated with another type of glue so that you could make up the sheet required for the size of the panel required before they were put in the press. The panels were trimmed and cut to the size required and inlaid with a narrow strip of black and white inlay to the pattern required.

Many of these panels were curved and shaped to the place where they had to fit in the coached. Curved doors and fittings also were made up. This was very interesting and exacting work and I became quite proficient at it. I was sorry then I had to leave this part of the plant to go into the coach shop.

In the coach shops we installed the new partitions, repaired other parts of the equipment and put up the fancy moldings and fittings that were the vogue in those times. As well as working on the wooden parts of the coaches I spent some time on the steel work on the outside and the frame of the coaches. This work was very interesting also as we had to bend and shape the steel plated to the various shapes required to fit the place it had to go. The outside plates had to be put up without any marks and the rivets had to be driven without marking up the plates. While I was working in the steel gang we built some of the semi open top observation cars that were put on the fun run through the mountains. These were the forerunners of the dome cars that are used today. When the dome cars came in to use these cars were taken off and put in to other service.

One apprentice before me had been put in the wood mill for a time but he had cut off part of his finger with the machines. This put a damper on the boys going into the mill for training for a while. The apprentice supervisor came to me one day and asked me if I would like to go in to the mill I said that I would like to have the chance to learn how to operate the machines so he said, "O.K. we will let you try it for now if you get cut or loose any fingers no more boys will go in there". So with that pleasant thought in mind I went on my merry way into the land of cut off fingers and thumbs. There were only one or two men who had spent their life in this work that didn't have one or two fingers missing. This was quite a large shop as they had many different and special machines that was able to handle and work the forty-foot timbers that were used in building the freight cars. I did my hitch in there without an accident so from then on this was part of the boys training. This was were I finished up the last of my apprenticeship so in September of 1928 I was handed my mechanics certificate and given two years seniority on the seniority list.

During the five years of our apprentice we had to go to the company school. We took an I.C.S. course in the trade that we were taking. The examination sheets were taken out of the books that were in the back of them so that you couldn't just bone up on the answers. Mr. Bristol was the teacher, a very clever man, but a strict disciplinarian. We had to do our studying at home, then we attended classes in the Company schoolroom two hours once a week. In class we wrote the exams and did our drafting. Mr. Bristol would explain any of the parts of the course that we were having trouble with during class that was a big help. We had to finish a certain amount of work every month and our results were put up on a big board in the schoolroom so you could see how you stood in relation to the rest of the class.

After the first year, when I caught up on the mathematics that I had missed in public school, I usually was able to keep in the top ten of our class of about thirty-five boys. There was no shirking in this school because if you didn't do your work as required, Mr. Bristol could have you fired. At that time, the C.N.R. had the finest apprentice training programs in Canada. Most of the top Officials came from men who had been trained in this way. That is in the Mechanical Department. Judging from what I saw of the education of my two sons who attended University, I would say that we had about the equivalent of a First Year University training in the sciences of the trade that we were studying.

In April of 1923, my father left the shops where he worked as a Carmen's helper. He looked after the lumberyard for the Freight Car shop. He had a little shack with a stove in it that was kind of an office. He used to keep track of all the lumber that the men would take as they repaired the cars. Why he left this good job for him he didn't tell us.

Many years later I found out when I was visiting the shops as an official from the P.G.E. Railway. I was having lunch with some of the officials who were young men when my father worked in the lumberyard. The talk got around to the old days, and jocularly they mentioned that he was the only bootlegger that the C.N.R. had ever had on the property. I kept the conversation going on this tack and I found out that he kept a bottle or two in the shack. When the men came out for lumber they could buy a drink from him during working hours. The company found out and he was fired, as this is a violation of Rule G that prohibits the consumption of liquor on the company premises and is a dismissible offense for which the union cannot bring up as a grievance.

In May of 1923 he decided to go back to the farm near Pilot Mound that he still owned. As Tom had started my apprenticeship my brother Bill persuaded him to let us stay behind, so my parents along with my sister Susan went back there to live. They sold the house in Transcona and I went to live with my brother Tom and his wife.

I earned 25 cents an hour that came to about $42 a month, as we worked five and a half days a week at that time. I paid Tom $30 a month for board and $5 a month on the mortgage payments on Dad's house that he had sold. This left me about $7 a month to buy my clothes and for amusement, etc. So, from the age of sixteen on I was on my own. We received a raise of 2 and a half cents an hour every six months, but for the first two years I had to go home in threshing time and earn enough money working on a threshing outfit in order to buy my clothes.

When my parents left for the farm in 1923 about May, I was on my own at the age of sixteen and had to look out for myself, which I did from then on. I first went to stay with Tom and Agnes but as she was expecting a baby I had to find a place to board, so after awhile I went to live with a Scottish Family named Hayes. I stayed there for over a year. They had a piano and that is where I started to pick out tunes and chords on the piano.

While I was there I developed a hernia from the work I was doing in the shop. This called for a visit to the doctor and as I had never been to a doctor before I was somewhat scared. He told me I had to have an operation and as it was on compensation, he arranged a date for me to go into the St. Boniface Hospital. Now these people were quite superstitious. At supper that evening after I had come back from the doctor she asked the family if anyone had heard the dog howling last night for such a long time. Her husband said, "Ai. There's bound to be a death in the neighborhood." This remark lowered my already state of depression some more. However I didn't tell them that I had to go into the hospital until the next weekend as the operation was set up for Monday morning. When I told her she said, "Oh. You poor wee laddie, now I know why the dog was barking that night". Now in those days you only went to the hospital when you were just about ready to kick the bucket, operations were much more rare than they are today. I was only 17 years old when I walked into the hospital all by myself with the unknown before me. To make it worse, the priest came around just before you went to sleep to hear your confession so you would be already for the Pearly Gates if the surgeon's knife slipped the next day. So with all these comforting thoughts I climbed aboard the operating table the next morning. A very scared boy. However, as I was going under the anesthetic I kept saying to myself, "I'll beat that damn dog. I'll beat that damn dog". And of course I did.

Eric all dressed up in Transcona.

From the Hayes I went to stay with a family called Potter. In this menagerie there were Father and mother Potter and four male sons, another boarder, and myself. Eight people in all. Every day we knew what we were going to get to eat as she had a menu for each day and it never varied. However, we had lots of it so got along fairly well. I had to sleep in the same bed with the other boarder. We shared one room and the same bed. Now this man was a painter in the shops, He was a little man in late forties. He had always been a bachelor and was very much of an introvert. He used to read cheap paperback books most of the time, the majority of which were love stories. Sometimes during the night I would wake up with me being the object of his affections. Now don't misunderstand, he wasn't a homosexual, but just a lonely little man who had never had the love of a woman as he was too shy. However, these times were somewhat embarrassing as I would have to wake him up and he would be most apologetic. So I started to look around for another place to stay. By then Bill and Gladys had moved into a new house and there was room for me to stay with them, so I moved in with them and stayed with them until I was married. They were very good to me and made my life more homelike.

In my early teens one of my best friends was a lad of my own age, Bill Oliver. He was a machinist apprentice and lived quite close to me when I was living at my brother's place. The reader may wonder what we did for amusement at that time in a teenager's life when they are most likely to get into trouble. Well we didn't have much money to spend after your board was paid for so we made our own fun. In the summer we played a lot of pickup games of baseball on an empty lot. We went to the public swimming pool in Winnipeg where you could swim all day for twenty-five cents. We played a lot of card games and in the winter we skated and played a lot of hockey. About this time I bought my banjo and started to learn to play it. I started to take banjo lessons but trying to learn music was not for me so I quit before very first ten lessons were finished. Vaudeville was in its heyday at the time, so Bill and I would go to a show on Saturday after payday and there we would hear the latest songs. As by that time I had learned some ukulele chords, I tuned my banjo to ukulele tuning and as I had a good ear we would come from one of the shows with the tune in our heads then make up the chords to fit the tunes. I may not have had all the correct chords, but to us they seemed all right.

Two other lads, Bill and I, formed a little band and we played for whist drives and dance evenings at the local halls. They were all the rage in those days and the music we played included a lot of Scottish dances that were very much like the square dances that are dance today. We had a lot of fun at these evenings and that is without any liquor. People seemed to be able to enjoy themselves without liquor then, no doubt they couldn't afford it and it was hard to get after Prohibition.

In my later teens and after we were married I got in with another group who we more proficient and we took on engagements in Winnipeg playing for old time dances, club smokers, and party's were we also put on skits along with the music which usually included some member of the audience. I met a lot of people this way and began to become better known in the area.

One winter a machinist apprentice pal of ours bought a chassis of a Model T Ford. We all went in to Winnipeg to get it and we drove it home to his place with the four of us sitting on the gas tank and on a board across the frame. It was about ten below so we were just about frozen when we finally got it into his garage. During that winter we under slung the chassis and built a racing car body on it. I worked on the body and the machinists souped up the engine put twin exhaust pipes on it and we painted it yellow with black trim. We had a lot of fun building this car and a lot of free lunches from his mother. It was a big day when we took it out for it first trip. We had to take turns riding with the owner as it was only a single-seater like you see in the old movies with no doors on the side, just curved armrests cut in the side of the car covered with leather.

At this time I also had a friend who owned a motorcycle. I picked up a worn out old thing for a few dollars but I could never get it going. However I had many a ride on the back of his and on one of his friends who owned a big four-cylinder Harley Davidson Police bike. This was a lot of fun for a while until one Sunday morning I was driving this big bike down the back lane behind his place when I hit a bunch of chickens, silly things to be out on the lane on a Sunday morning. However, unbeknown to me was the owners pride and joy, a huge red rooster which I found out had to be killed. Any way on Monday morning, Jack Richards the friend who owned the bike and whose place we were at came to me in to the shop and told me that the man who owned the rooster came over to his dad after we had gone and said that he had reported to the R.C.M.P. that a tall fellow wearing a brown turtle necked sweater had killed his rooster. That was I. That afternoon as I was coming out of a coach I was working in I saw a Mountie going in to the shop office. Now I had visions of me being led off in chains to Stony mountain, the local rock pile for criminals. I made myself scarce in another part of the shops. However he evidently did not come for me as he took off after a while. But that was the end of my motorcycle career as I didn't have a bike of my own and I wasn't going to go back to Jack's place.

One Saturday evening I along with a group of young fellows were invited to a house party. It was held at the home of girl named Mary Uhrich. After I was introduced to her I found out that she was the little blond girl in my Grade 8 class who was very shy and did not speak up when the teacher asked to read out aloud. We had lost track of one another since school days and she had changed from a shy little mouse into a lovely young lady. I had a wonderful time at the party and the rest of the family especially her mother made us all feel at home so much that some how or other on saying good night I forgot my rubber overshoes. Of course, I had to go back there a few days later to get them, after a pleasant evening I asked her for a date and from then on we went on many dates together.

I was eighteen very close to nineteen at that time so a group of young men and girls that we all know formed a club called The Jolly Glee Club. There were enough of us that we could hire a hall and put on our own dances, snowshoe party's toboggan party at the big toboggan run in RiverPark at that time, which was much like a roller coaster but the slides were ice runways which finally spilled you out on to the river bed. With about ten or twelve boys and girls on a huge toboggan you got up to quite a speed coming off the shutes and usually ended up in a mass of tangled arms and logs on the river ice. Of course if you were holding on to your girl friend this was the time that you got in the extra hug and kiss, even if she was all bundled up and had a cold nose that felt like an icicle. This took the place of skiing that is one of the favorite sports of the young people today. At that time skiing as it is done to day was not available to the young people.

Winter sports – snowshoeing Rose, Eric, and Mary.

In the summer we would go as a club to Grand Beach, a summer resort on Lake Winnipeg about fifty miles north east of Winnipeg. These were good outings as we could swim in the lake from a clean white sand beach, have a picnic supper that the girls would provide then dance to a good band in the large pavilion on the boardwalk by the beach. Then it was in to the train and the journey home. I was quite the popular fellow on the way home as I knew how to get into the switchbox and turn off most of the lights in our coach. This improved the ride home with your girl, but was frowned upon by the conductor.

In the summer we would quite often go on a family picnic with Ma and Pa Uhrich and the rest of the family and whoever wanted to was welcome to come along. It was always Pa's job to supervise the big bonfire get it ready to roast the potatoes, corn, or whatever was on the menu. As the countryside around Winnipeg was quite unsettled we only had to go about thirty miles or so until we had a private place to ourselves, either by the side of the Brokenhead river or out in the Bird Hill District where there was lots of empty space. After a swim in the river or a ball game or other diversions, we would gather around the bonfire and eat our supper of many other things but always the roast potatoes or corn covered with butter until it ran down your arm and off your elbow. These were happy times indeed for the Uhrich family and friends.

Soon after I started going out with Mary, Tom Acres started going out with her sister Rose, who is about a year younger than Mary. He bought a 1920 Chevrolet four door sedan, so the four of us used to go out together all the time to shows, etc. He was a few years older than me and had a bad foot that gave him a permanent limp. He was a good hunter and he took me out on quite a few weekends and from him I learned how to shoot a shotgun. I must mention one of our hunting trips that we took. We took our holidays together with the object of going down to Detroit Lakes in Minnesota for some fishing, then be back in Manitoba for duck shooting.

Changing a flat tire on Tom Acres 1927 Chevrolet, Labor Day 1927.

We went across the border at Emerson, down through North Dakota and in to the Detroit Lake District. The place we were going to was out in the wilds with only a poor gravel road that you had to travel to get there. Before starting up this gravel road and as it was late in the afternoon; we stopped at the gas station at the junction, gassed up, and had a hamburger and a cup of coffee then started off up this trail. It was quite dark when we got to the lake but there was another fellow there who had been fishing and was just leaving.

After some conversation as to who we were and where we came from as he could tell we were not Americans by the car license, he asked us if we had bought our fishing license before we came in. We said no, we don't need a license to fish in Manitoba. "Well bub", he said to Tom. "You sure do in this country and before you wet a line you had better go along this trail apiece and get one off the game warden who was in his cabin down the trail. We thanked him for his advice and he took off down the road that we had come in. As we had eaten before we came in we took off down the trail to find the game warden as we didn't want to get pinched for fishing without a license.

We found the log shack by the glimmer of the coal oil light through the window and knocked on the door. A tall outdoorsy man opened the door so after explaining what we had

73

come for he invited us in and made us some coffee and we spent the rest of the evening talking fishing and hunting and got our licenses then went back to the car. We had no sleeping bags so we spent the night on the ground under our blankets. Now I mean under, as the mosquitos were so thick that was the only way you could get any sleep at all. Needless to say we didn't got much sleep and got up in the morning groggy and bitten. It was a lovely lake and there were boats there that we had paid the warden for the use of them, so after breakfast we got our tackle together and started fishing.

The lake was full of fish. Black and Rainbow Bass. The water was crystal clear so you could see down into the water for a long way. The fish were so plentiful that immediately you put your baited hoot down into the water the fish took it. They were quite small so after awhile it was just a matter of trying to catch the biggest fish out of the school that was swimming around your bait. I do not exaggerate at all when I say this as it is hard to believe in these days or overfishing of our lakes and streams that fish could be so plentiful.

We went in for lunch about noon, filleted a bunch of these fish then cooked them over our campfire and then sat around in the shade smoking and having a little snooze. Tom could sleep anywhere. I have been out with him on duck hunts sleeping on the bare ground. I would be tossing and turning while he would be blissfully unconscious snoring away even if we were sleeping on hard ground or roots.

I was awake when I heard a car coming up the hill to the lake. It pulled up along side of us and stopped. Two state troopers got out complete with revolvers on their belts that I noticed where unfastened. That is I mean the flaps were open ready for action. They said, "Howdy men, what are your names and where do you come from". So we told them who we were and where we worked what we were doing down here so far from Canada, and that we were on holidays. Tom produced his driver's license and told them that it was his car. They were not at all a chummy couple of lads and kept their distance when they were plying us with questions.

The hunters – Eric Stathers left and Tom Acres right.

Then came the bombshell. "Where were you last evening about nine o'clock? Why we were here setting up camp," we replied. "How do we know that", they said. "Well there was a man in here when we came in and he was talking to us." "Where is he now?", they asked. "Well he took off soon after we came in", we said. "He went down the road you came in", and we described the car he was driving. "Have you no other proof that you were here than that", they asked. So I said, "What's the matter Officer, what have we done that you are asking us all these questions for". "Never mind if you have no more proof than that you will have to come with us", he said. Then I thought of the Ranger that we bought our license off so I told them that we had bought our licenses from the Ranger who had a line cabin down the road apiece. He said, "Get in", so we all climbed in to the police car and went down to the ranger's cabin. Thank the lord he was there. The police evidently knew him as they addressed him by his first name. They asked him if we had bought fishing licenses off him last night and at what time. He told them and also said that we had spent most of the, evening with him. So he asked the officers what was the matter. They said, "Those two men are lucky you were here with them last night as the man who runs the garage at the turn off into the lake was held up last night ,shot and killed by two men who these two, meaning us answer the description to. So you see we could have been taken in on a murder charge as that was the man who gassed up our car and where we had the meal before we started up the road in. "Whew", I still feel grateful to that ranger as justice was pretty shaky in those days as there was a lot of booze run down to the States over the same route that we came in mostly by young Canadian fellows like we were, and they were not too popular with the state police.

Well that kind of ruined the day for us, so after supper we hit upon a plan to beat the mosquitoes. We tied the two boats together with two poles and saddled then out in to the other end of the lake, made up our bed in the bottom of the boats and blissfully were rocked off to sleep. I woke up from a dream that I was drowning and I could feel the water on my face. I looked up over the side of the boat and there was a thunderstorm coming up and the waves were sloshing in to the boat. Of course, Tom was fast asleep. I got up and shook him awake and we pulled the anchor and started to paddle to the shore. Luckily the wind was blowing us in to the part of the lake where we camped. By the time we had got near the shore it was all we could do to keep the boats from turning sideways and getting swamped. We landed on the shore in a downpour of rain and made a dash for the car. We got inside the car, me in the back and Tom in the front seat watching the lightning flash and the wind whip up huge waves on the lake. Then came a big crash and the tree that we had been sitting under during the day came down in front of the car, some of the branches hitting the front of the hood. Well we spent another sleepless night as we tried to sleep In the car for the rest of it. Tom did okay, but me no way.

We had our breakfast as soon as it got light enough, cleared away the top of the tree so we could got out, then decided that Detroit Lakes was not the place for us so we headed back to the border and home.

In September of 1927 Gladys and Bill, Mary and I went to the farm where Dad and Mom was, which was the old original farm that was in the Pembina Valley which is really nice country. One night when there was a big moon I took Mary out for a walk along the edge of the prairie where you could look over the valley. The grain had been freshly cut in the field where we were walking giving off an aroma of fresh cut ripe hay which is a perfume that you have experience to appreciate it. We stopped and looked out over the valley that was lit up like day, I would say a most romantic setting. I put my arms around her, told her how much I loved her and asked her to marry me. After a little while I suppose this was the proper thing to do then, keep the suitor waiting on edge for awhile, any way before we got back to the house she had consented, but we both agreed that I had to finish my apprenticeship first, which would be some time in 1928.

Mary Uhrich, Eric Stathers, Rose Uhrich, and Tom Acres in Winnipeg park 1928.

When we came home I bought her a diamond engagement ring. I got it from Birks in Winnipeg and it cost me a little more than three weeks wages at that time. She still has it. I wonder what it would be worth today in 1975. I won't bore you with more of the family doings, but Mary and I, Tom and Rose went out together more often than before as he became engaged to Rose soon after. Mary and I made our plans as time went along for our marriage. We rented an upstairs in an old house on Spence Street that was partially furnished and as the marriage was set for September 1, 1928 We took it from that date on, as Mary wanted to keep working at her job after we married.

On September 1, 1928 Mary and I were married in the Uhrich family home. The minister was the Lutheran Pastor the Reverend Weigner. We went into Winnipeg to have the wedding pictures taken, then we came back to the house where the wedding reception was held. The house was crowded with guests, from both sides of the family and also some of my friends from the shops. My father's greeting to my new bride as soon as the ceremony was over was, "Well you're alright now old girl you've caught your bus".

Eric Stathers 1928

Now it was the custom of the time to have a chivaree for the bride and groom after they had gone to bed but seeing as we had a suite in the city our friends could not do this as they would have been taken in for disturbing the peace. Now a chivaree was a gathering of some of the exuberant guests who equipped themselves with pots and cans and any other type of container that they could bang upon. They would go to the unlucky couples place of abode, stand outside their window, and make the most noise they could interlaced with bawdy jokes until the newlyweds had to come down and let them in and provide them with liquid refreshments. Sometimes in their exuberance they have been, known to kidnap either one of the couple and not take him or her back until morning.

Mary Stathers 1928

So seeing that they couldn't do that, here is what we had to go through. As we had no car one of our friends was slated to drive us into the city from Transcona after the reception was over. On our way to the city he ran out of gas. Some twerp had drained his gas tank and he and I were just starting to walk about two miles into the nearest gas station when who should come along but one of the other guests. So he drove us into town and we got enough gas to proceed on our way. When we got to our house on Spence Street the usual goodnights were said and they took off.

We unlocked the front door and quietly went into the house so as not to wake up the landlord who lived in the downstairs part. Good Lord! The stairs that we had to go up were all interlaced with rope and tied with double knots which I had to untie to get up the stairs, however we managed to get enough off so we could crawl through and we opened up the door to the suite. Wow! The kitchen furniture was in the living room and the living furniture was in the kitchen. So we said so what, we can fix that in the morning, lets got ready for bed. Mary went into the bathroom to get ready and I undressed in the bedroom. I pulled my new pajamas out of the drawer and they were full of dried peas, which rolled all over the floor. Did you ever try walking over dried peas in your bare feet on a cold floor? I scraped as many as I could into a corner of the room, put on my pajamas, and sat down on the edge of the bed. Tinkle, tinkle. Someone had wired a sheep bell to the spring mattress under the bed, so I had to find a pair of pliars and crawl under the bed on the dried peas and get it off. By this time Mary had finished her toilet and came in to the room and found me lying under the bed muttering to myself as I was trying to get off the bell. "What are you doing down there dear?", she asked. "We are supposed to sleep together in the bed, not in and under?" This brought some smart remarks from me as finally I managed to get the bell off.

So finally we get into bed. We were so tired that we lay there just relaxing. It was very quiet in the rooms as it was early in the morning and the city traffic had not started to move yet. "Do you hear that noise dear?" Mary said. So I listened and sure enough I could hear something ticking somewhere in the suite. Up on to the cold floor again in my bare feet. Damn those peas, I said to myself as I walked around the place trying to locate the noise. Finally I found it. It was in one of the hot air registers behind the grill in the kitchen. I needed a big screwdriver to take off the grill and as I didn't have one I said, "To Hell with it let it go off when it wants too", so promptly at four o'clock it went off and woke up the whole house. Fun and games as was played on newlyweds in those days.

Being somewhat of an old square, and seeing that what I want to say is rather personal, I am somewhat hesitant in writing the next few lines. However, I think that young people of today whose moral code differs from that in which we were brought up in, and indulge in sexual experiences in the back seat of cars and other places of a like nature, miss one if not the most ecstatic experiences of life. When two people like Mary and I who loved one another, even though we knew all the score, have during their courtship denied themselves of the final stage of sex, come together after they are married and in ideal surroundings and with no feeling of regret or guilt afterward give their bodies to one another, not with just lust, but with love and affection, have something that they can look back on for the rest of their lives. That is our feeling on this much-discussed subject.

We went back to the farm for a two week honeymoon, then on our return we settled down to be married folks and working for a living. Mary kept on with her job at Eaton's and I commuted daily to Transcona shops. We both had a long walk to catch the train and the bus; on the cold winter mornings these walks were not very much appreciated. However we had many happy times by ourselves, window shopping along Portage Avenue, going to shows about once a week, and outings with the family.

When I was married I was working in the wood mill as a wood machinist. That is I was running any of the various machines that the foreman put me on. I had to leave there on account of another man with more seniority than I, wanted the job, so I was sent to the repair track. This is where the cars from the running yards are sent for light repairs. All the work is done outdoors in all kinds of weather. The month of January 1928-29 was one of the coldest months ever recorded in Winnipeg up to that time. The average temperature for the month was fifteen below zero. We worked outside in as low a temperature as forty below zero. We had to build screens of grain doors and wood to keep the wind off us otherwise it was impossible to work with the cars sometimes with bare hands. I was with the steel gang, working under the cars installing brake parts. I had to use the riveting gun and my hands would freeze with the cold air going through the gun, then my neck was covered with small burns, as the hot scale from the cinder hot rivets would fall down between the upturned collar of my sheepskin coat and my neck.

Being out in that extreme cold all day had the effect that as soon as I got home and in to the warm house I would get sleepy and after supper it was almost impossible to keep awake. I guess that I wasn't much company for my young wife during that time. In March there was another opening in the wood mill so I got my old job back again were I was much happier with the working conditions. At that time mechanics working, on Freight Cars received 63 cents an hour and mechanics working on Passenger cars and millwork received 69 cents an hour. We worked five and sometimes five and one half days a week with no overtime for Saturday morning.

Our rent for the suite was thirty-five dollars a month. We didn't spend much on amusement and nothing on liquor as neither of us would drink at all then so we were able to put aside a nice little saving. Besides that we were both working. We wanted to go back to Transcona and buy a little house that I could add on to and improve we went along. In April of 1929 we had the chance to buy a little cottage just behind the Uhrich's house so we took it. We got it for $1200, $200 down, and $25 a month. The people that owned it had been very good friends of Ma Uhrich so they didn't charge us any interest on the balance. I think that was their way of trying to pay Ma back for all the things she had done for them when they were married and their kids started coming along.

It was just a little place sitting on cement blocks with no basement. It had a kitchen with a pantry, a small dining room, a small living room, and one bedroom. There was no bathroom as there was no water down that street so we had to get our water either from the community pump at the corner of the block, or from the Uhrich's house across the lane. The privy was at the back near the back lane sitting on a cement tank. Every so often the town employees with what we called the honey-wagon emptied it. This was a horse drawn wagon with an open wooden tank on it. There was a back door to the privy which they opened and ladled the contents of the tank into the wagon. Phooey! You could tell when it was coming a block away depending on the prevailing wind.

We bought some furniture, a kitchen table two chairs, a small cheap dining room suite with four chairs, and the Toronto couch that we still have and sits on the veranda at Gun Lake, for the living room. For the bedroom Mary loaned her bed and dresser from her Ma so with some bedding and pots and pans on the first of May we moved into our own house. I started a garden in the yard digging up the tough prairie sod, that was quite a task.

A little while later on I picked up an old model T Ford two-door sedan for $200. This enabled us to get around and join in the family picnics, etc. It wasn't much of a car, however, it served our purpose. So there we were at the age of twenty-two very happy with our own house, and car ready to become stable citizens of Transcona.

I think that this is a good place to come to the end of the first part of my story. I have tried to show how we lived in the parts of Manitoba that we went to. I could have elaborated in detail many of the experience that we went through and told of many more incidents that were of great importance to me and mine, but to avoid boring the reader with a lot of stories that the reader may not enjoy reading I have left them out. So as a lot of the old time stories end, we got married and lived happily every after. This page was written on December 23, 1975 and includes our wedding photograph on September 1, 1928.

Eric and Mary Stathers 1928, September 1, 1928

5. BRITISH COLUMBIA

Transcona, July 1929. I woke up this summer morning to the sound of the 6:45 a.m. shop whistle telling us, "Get up lads it is time to get ready to go to work". I lay there for a minute or two with the thought that some how or other this day was going to be different than the regular run of days that our life was getting in to. Mary said, "Don't you think that it is time to get going so with that encouragement I arose, we had our breakfast, and I toddled off to work in the wood mill in the C.N.R. Railway shops.

During the morning the shop steward a Mr. Cameron passed by my machine that I was running and told me to come and see him at lunchtime. As I was on the shop grievance committee for the Carmen's Union at the time I thought to myself "Oh, oh", another gripe about something that we will have to take up with management, so with that thought in mind at noon I took my lunch up to the cabinet where he worked and sat on his bench and ate my lunch while he talked.

Well it wasn't a gripe that he wanted to see me about at all. Instead he told me that he had been asked to recommend to management an ex-carman apprentice to them who would become the car apprentice supervisor, to work with management and the apprentices to see that they were rotated in the various branches of the trade so that they would have the best training available. The duties were in the shops. I would only have to take Mr. Bristol's place if he was sick or absent.

He asked me if I would like to have the job. If so he would put up my name for the position. I thought for awhile as this was a new position they were establishing in the shop and it could either be abolished at a later date or could be the stepping stone to a foreman's job or better. When he assured me that if I didn't make a go of it or the job was abolished, I could go back to my old place in the mill I accepted with thanks and he said that he would put my name to the management for their choice for the job.

I went back to work elated as this meant that I would get away from the monotony of the machine work. I would be on a salary and more or less on my own and the only supervision that I would have would be the results that I could produce. It was a challenge. I could hardly wait to get home to tell Mary about it.

A couple of days passed when one afternoon the foreman came down from the office and told me that Mr. Bristol wanted to see me in the apprentice's classroom. As he would always stop and chat with me whenever we ran across one another in the shop area, I thought that maybe he wants a little job done for the school which had been the reason that I had been asked to go a couple times before.

He told me to sit down and passed the usual remarks about the weather, etc. Then he threw the bombshell at me. "How would you like to go to British Columbia and take a car foreman's job with the Pacific Great Eastern Railway in their shops at Squamish", he said. I guess I must have looked bewildered as I had never even heard of the P.G.E. or even thought of leaving the C.N.R. service, especially as I had just been recommended for apprentice supervisor's job.

He then went on to describe the little village of Squamish, how pretty it was situated on the coast with the snow-capped mountains all around it. He described it in such glowing terms that I began to imagine some sort of a Shangri-La. It seemed that the locomotive foreman of the P.G.E. was an old buddy of his from England as they had served their apprenticeship together with one of the English Railways. Evidently Mr. Bailey the Locomotive foreman was visiting them in Winnipeg and had asked him to recommend someone for the job and he would be out to Transcona shops the next day to interview the man he would recommend.

I asked Mr. Bristol why he picked on me for the job. He said to me. "Eric, I remember the day you came in to write you examination for to get in to be an apprentice, how you failed that exam and when I gave you another chance you did an excellent job of it". "I have watched you grow up from a boy into a young man and I am sure that you will be able to do just as good a job in this opportunity as you have done for me here". I thanked him very kindly for his confidence, in me and told him that I would have to talk it over with my wife before I could give him the answer. Any way I would come and meet the man the next day if he would arrange it with my foreman.

When I got home I told Mary what had happened and asked her what she thought. She said, "This may be our opportunity, it only knocks once, if we don't go and have a look we may ever after be sorry". We went over to tell her folks and get their thinking on our going away. Pa said in his easy way, "Don't go so far away, it rains out there so much that you will get webbed feet and moss on your backs". Ma remarked quietly. "Do you have to go so far away?" But neither of them said, "Don't

84

go".

The next afternoon I got the message to go to the classroom and there I met Mr. Bailey. He was a handsome man with dark curly hair and a jolly manner. He had only the index finger left on his right hand. He had been in an accident at work and his hand had been crushed so badly that all the doctors could save was the one finger with most of the palm gone.

He told me about the job, the shops and the town and climate. He thought that the P.G.E. was going places and that it may be taken over by the C.N.R. That was why he had left his job with the C.N.R. in New Westminster about a year ago and went to the P.G.E. as Locomotive Foreman.

Seeing that we had two weeks holiday coming up within a week, I said that I would come up to Squamish along with my wife if transportation could be arranged. Mr. Bristol said that he could look after that so we parted saying to each other, we will see you in Squamish soon. Inside of a few days a pass to Vancouver over the C.N.R, was delivered to me so Mary and I made our preparations to go to the coast. This was to be a big adventure as neither of us had ever seen a mountain in our lives.

One of the friends of the family and a good friend and confident of mine was a man who I had worked with in the shops. His name was Tommy Quail. He was a bachelor but had been married and divorced and had led quite a varied life. Before we made up our mind to go to B.C, I had a long talk with him about the advisability of taking the job in Squamish. His only comment was that he thought that I would not have trouble with the technical part of the job but seeing that I was so young I might have trouble with discipline with men that were a lot older than myself, However, if I remembered that I would be on the other side of the fence and I did not associate too much with the men when I was off the job I should be able to make a go of it. However as he was going to Vancouver on his holidays to stay with some friends of his, we could go along with him and he would show us around Vancouver.

We left Winnipeg in the evening on the C.N.R. We installed ourselves into a lower berth in a tourist class sleeping car. As we were both skinny then we could both squeeze in to one berth and, as we hadn't been married to long why we didn't mind the squeezing part too much anyway. The tourist class sleepers then gave you a comfortable four-place seat with an upper and lower berth.

If you didn't take the whole sector, you maybe would have to share the seats with whoever had the upper berth. There was a little kitchen in one end of the car where you could make light meals, a cup of tea, or anything you wanted if you brought your own food and dishes along. At the other end of the car was a large combined men's washroom and smoking room as smoking was not allowed in the main part of the car and as women very rarely smoked then this was where the men congregated and swapped yarns and drinks out of the bottles that they had brought along for medicinal purposes. Drinking in public was very much a no-no and the bottles were kept out of sight in case the conductor came along. This provided a meeting place for the travelers and it wasn't very long until every one in the car got acquainted with each other.

We didn't sleep much the first night on the train as we were exited with our new adventure and the clickety clack, clickety clack of the wheels going over the joints in the rails kept us awake. Once in awhile the train would come to a stop and as the slack ran in along the train you would be thrown up against the end of the berth with a jolt, which further added to your trouble in getting a sound sleep. Trains then did not run so smoothly as they do today. The whole of the next day we were running through the prairies of Saskatchewan, but on the second day we were in the foothills of Alberta and we were eagerly looking for our first sight of the mountains. Then in the distance we could see what we thought were white clouds on the horizon. Someone in the car said, "There is the mountains". As we drew nearer to them and finally were running through them, we were awed by the size of them and what we were seeing on each side of the train as we drew nearer to the town of Jasper.

On the way to Vancouver by Train from Transcona taken at Blue River in 1929.

We stopped for quite a while at Jasper as the train was switched around various cars added or taken off and one of the partially open observation cars of the type that I had help to build in Transcona was put on the rear end of the train. We had our picture taken by the Totem pole that was near the station then it was all aboard for Vancouver and we were off again. We were surprised by the difference between the placid rivers of the prairies that we had been used to compared to the turbulent rushing streams and rivers with their boiling waters falling over the black rocks and through the canyons on their way to the ocean.

On the way to Vancouver by train at Jasper near the train platform.

As we came nearer to the coast we saw the big trees and the jungle like vegetation so different to what we had been brought up in. We arrived in Vancouver in the morning and there to meet us were Tommy and his friends the Fosters. After being introduced all round we all piled in to their car that was a very ancient Chevy touring car with a cloth top, that banged and clattered its way out to their place that was in the bush where 21st Street and McDonald are located now. They were poor people and were building their house by themselves. It was only partially finished but livable. They were down to earth people who didn't have much, but you were made to feel welcome to what they had and were a very happy and jolly family. Mr. Foster had been with Tommy in the First World War and he worked for the city as a laborer. They were not too well off as they had two young hoys to feed as well.

The Foster's car in Vancouver with goats on the hood.

It was quite a menagerie as they kept chickens; rabbits, goats and I think they had some ducks and geese as well as that part Vancouver at that time was not developed and part of their property was quite wet. The reason I mention these people is that we owed them a debt for the things they did for us later on and as we were only a friend of their friend it shows how big hearted these people were.

We stayed at the Fosters for a couple of days and saw some of the sights of Vancouver, then the next morning we went to the Union Steamship dock that was at the foot of Carroll street and got aboard the Lady Alexandria. We were very interested in the goings on at the dock. The boat was been loaded with all kinds of freight and material for the places of call on its trip up the sound to Squamish. The different kinds of people that were coming up the gang plank, from loggers in their rough clothes with their caulked shoes hanging around their necks to the tourists in their classy clothes and cameras hanging around their necks.

We weren't too impressed with the smell of the ocean as it was flavored with the smell of numerous floating objects and garbage covering the water by the side of the boat. However, when we backed out into the harbor and got on our way we were very much impressed with the view of Stanley Park shoreline and the mountains on the north shore. As we headed out in to the open water we got the first real smell of the sea. There was no First Narrows Bridge then so we could see right out to Vancouver Island. It was a beautiful bright summers day. Mary and I stayed on deck all the time, as we didn't want to miss anything and as we rounded Point Atkinson and saw the Sound with sail boats, speedboats and other pleasure craft dotting the water we seemed to be sailing in to a green paradise where everyone was on holidays.

We continued on to Bowen Island and tied up at the dock in a little bay that we were told was called Snug Cove. People were waiting on the dock for the boat to come in, to meet friends and relatives coming to the island. There were many shouts of greeting as people got off the boat and what with the noise of the winches and the crew unloading cargo on to the dock it was a scene of happy confusion. We gathered that this was a holiday resort as there was a number of pleasure craft tied up in the cove and children rowing around the water and playing on the sandy beach at the end of the cove.

This was a most charming and pretty place but as soon as the unloading was finished, the boat blew its whistle, backed out of the cove and we were on our way again. We had gone along for a short distance, when a young man in white coat came around the boat with what looked like a four-note xylophone on one arm and hitting the notes with the other. This got all the passengers attention and he announced that this was the first call for dinner.

We then went off the deck and in to the main salon where there was a wide set of stairs leading down in the dining room under the salon. At the bottom of the stairs stood the steward who asked me for my ticket when we got opposite him. I pilled out the stub from my fare ticket but was told that I had to go up to the purser's office and buy a meal ticket for dinner. So back up I went and for seventy-five cents each I received a ticket for the meal. When I returned to the dining room Mary was seated at one of the tables so I took a seat along side of her. There was a snow-white tablecloth on the table with nice chinaware on it. There were linen napkins and an array of silver ware opposite each place. The furniture was all mahogany and the interior of the room was furnished in elegant taste with carpet on the floor.

Our waiter handed us the menu so for seventy five cents we had a starter of fish, either cod or salmon with lemon slices, the choice of two soups, with the main course of either roast beef with two vegetables or another kind of meat. The dessert was either pie or cake and cheese or some kind of pudding. Tea coffee or milk was the beverage and you could have as many refills as you wanted. After leaving a twenty-five cent tip for the waiter, Mary and I went back up on deck stuffed.

However after being on deck for a while and watching the coastline and the various islands go by we soon lost the stuffed feeling and were eagerly watching for the first site of Squamish. Soon we saw a group of grey buildings off to the right side of us but we were told this was Britannia Mines. We tied up to the dock at this place and quite a few men got off the boat here but they did not unload much cargo as we we were told that this was train day and they would unload on the way back. Then it was off again to a group of large buildings across the sound that they said was Woodfiber. Again they didn't stay long, just enough time to let the passengers off and a few crates of freight, and then it was on to Squamish.

As we left Woodfiber you could see the land at the end of the sound. There dominating the whole scene was this beautiful snow capped mountain, standing like a queen with her court far above the surrounding lower slopes. We were told that this mountain was Garibaldi and that Squamish was in back from the shoreline.

The Squamish boat dock 1930 with clear cuts on the hills below Mt. Garibaldi.

As we got near to the shore we could see that there were two long docks jutting out in to the water. One of these docks had a train standing on it, with the engine on the far end. On the other dock toward the falls that we could see coming down the mountain, were some men working and a car and a truck. We tied up at the dock that the train was on and then the people who were going on the P.G.E. got off the boat and boarded the train. The crew unloaded a quantity of freight and express which was out aboard the train as fast as it came off the boat.

We were told to wait until we went over to the other dock so after the unloading was finished the boat went over there and we got off and got in to a taxi that was driven by a Mr. Wallace. Another couple of people got in to the taxi and we drove off through an avenue of trees, which to us seemed to be for a long time, stopping only once at a large building on the left side of us which we were told that it belonged to a Mr. Galbraith and it used to be a hotel at one time. After we got further along just were the south end of where the Irly Bird yard is now we went over a wooden bridge and there before us was a double row of P.G.E. company cottages. A few other houses dotted what was then an immense lawn; it was all short grass with a few horses and cows grazing on it.

The company cottages lined both sides of the street. They were a very pretty site, as each little cottage had a beautiful flower garden, some with trellises with climbing roses and honeysuckle trailing all over them. You could smell the honeysuckle perfume as you went by. At the end of these houses was another bridge over a watercourse and then there was the main business district of the town that stretched for two blocks. There were two hotels, the Squamish Hotel where it is today and the Newport which was on the corner where the Chieftain Hotel is, along the two blocks with some houses in between were McKenzie's Store, Adams and Adams Groceries and Dry Goods, Kennedy's Hardware, Stan Clarke's gas pump and coal depot, a bake shop, a barber shop, the Post office, a restaurant, a couple of offices, another two large buildings that were vacant, and the Rex Theater where it is today. Further up the street where the Royal Bank is, were four small houses. Mr. Bailey lived in one of these along with his sister Mrs. Moon. That is were Mary went.

I got off at the station that was at the end of Main Street at the tracks. Mr. Baily was waiting there for me with a speeder to take me up to the shops. I was to look them over and meet Mr. Kyle the Master Mechanic in charge of the shops. We went up the track for a couple of miles then went back in to the shop area that was surrounded by bush on three sides. The shops consisted of the Boiler House, Roundhouse with turntable, Blacksmith shop, Car shop, Stores and a small office set apart from the main buildings. Of these buildings only the Car shop remains today.

Squamish railway shops 1929.

There was one set of tracks leading into the roundhouse area and another set of tracks leading into the car shop area, the car shop tracks divided into three tracks that went into the shop itself, and two tracks went on by the car shop down about three hundred feet which was the coach yard. Another track led off the coach yard that was used for storing the equipment used for the Sunday specials.

It was not an impressive sight for me coming from a huge sprawling complex of shop that I had been used to working in. However, Mr. Bailey took me in to the office where he introduced me to Mr. Kyle the Master Mechanic who was in charge of the Mechanical Department for the whole railroad. He was a rather large man with a florid complexion that I found out later as I started to work with him blossomed out to fiery red whenever he became angry. He asked me quite a few questions as to the type of work I was used too and if I had any experience in wrecking service. To the last question I had to answer no as the apprentices were not allowed to go out on wreck service at that time. He said that he thought that I could handle the job alright and as for the wrecking, if I would ask him or a carman called Alex McDonald when we went out on them any thing that I didn't understand what to do about it, I should make out O.K.

About the time we were through talking the shop whistle went and after the men went he and Mr. Bailey took me around the different shops. The round house had six stalls, one of them was floored over and was used as the machine shop with one or two lathes and various smaller machines scattered around.

The turntable was south of the roundhouse and was connected to each stall with six tracks. Beyond that was dense bush. There was a small shed east of the roundhouse housing the large wheel lathe and alongside of that was the wheel storage platform. In order to get the mounted wheels over and back to the car shop they had to be rolled up to the switch at the main line then back to the car shop by hand power. Then the blacksmith shop was east of the roundhouse between it and the car shop. The office was at the north end of the wheel storage platform. We went in to the blacksmith shop. The equipment in there consisted of two forges and anvils, one oil furnace, and a small steam hammer. At the back of this was a small lean-to where the brasses were babbited for the locomotive and cars.

Then into what was to be my domain. It was a high wooden building with three tracks. It would hold six cars as the wood working machinery, the pipe and tin shop, and the paint shop took up part of the place. There was no office for the foreman as he worked off a stand up desk in the north corner of the building. The floor was rough wood and it was heated by two large cast iron coal burning stoves, one at each end of the shop. I asked Mr. Kyle that if I took the job could I build a small office for myself in the north corner. This he agreed to and we went on to see the rest of the place including the stores, repair tracks, and coach yard.

Squamish railway car shop in 1929 with Eric Stathers standing.

The Repair Tracks and Coach Yard were very primitive, just tracks on hard packed gravel, but the coach yard had water pipe laid down along side of a wooden walk for about three hundred feet. There was no road into the shop so to get back to the town we took a trail that started from the south end of the roundhouse and wended its way through the bush, sometimes on wooden trestles over little gullies that I thought would be filled with water in the rainy season. I wasn't wrong in this thought, as I found out later. Mr. Kyle had an old Model T touring car with the top and side curtains parked at the end of the trail where it met the gravel road going up the valley, so we got into this old heap and started of in the direction of the town.

One of the first PGE refrigerator cars built in the Squamish shops.

We got out at Mr. Baileys house just north of Pemberton Road and there I met Mrs. Moon, Harold's sister and her daughter Grace. Mrs. Moon was a bustling very friendly woman who soon had us sitting down to a good supper, afterwards we sat on their back screened in veranda and got better acquainted. Harold, as I will call him from now on, for awhile said that as the hotel was rather a rough place for a young women to stay, we could spend the night with them and look for a place to stay in on the next day. This was readily accepted by so we stayed with them that night and the next one.

Mr. Bailey and his niece Grace showing us the village from Bughouse Heights.

The next day Mary and I started looking around town for a little house or an apartment for rent. It was pretty hopeless as every where we went we got the same story, full up, except for the two hotels and we couldn't afford to stay there as we had only about forty dollars left and our pass home. Near the end of the day we got a tip that a Mr. Kunts had a little shack that he rented and he lived on Third Street near the United Church. So over there we went and we met this person who showed us the shack.

Our first home in Squamish, a one room shack on Third Street behind the United Church.

We opened the door to the shack and I felt somewhat like my mother must have felt when she looked at the shack on the prairie for the first time. It was one room with a sleazy curtain at the back hiding a bed that sagged so much in the middle that when you both got in it you rolled into one lump in the middle with your bum about four inches off the floor and your head and feet about four inches above your tummy. The floor was rough fir board with cracks in between them that the mice could enter at will. There was a small kitchen table and two chairs and an easy chair with the legs partially sawn off, that put the seat so low to the floor that if you sat down too hard you would hit bottom. There were a few shelves on the end wall that held a collection of various dishes and pots, a sheet metal stove and an upturned orange grate with washbasin on it and a water pail along side that served as the bathroom. However as the rent was only eight dollars a week we said that we would take it and we would come in the next day and clean it up. So we went back to Harold's place for the night and the next day we set up house keeping in Squamish. Friday the Eighteenth day of July 1929.

As my appointment had to be approved by Mr. Robert Wilson the executive assistant who would be up at the shop on the Monday following, we had the weekend to ourselves. As we didn't know anyone in the town we took long walks all around the village and area. Mr. Bailey took us up on the Sunday to Bughouse Heights as it was called in those days. The reason for this name was that four or five people built houses up they're in the early Twenty's and people said they were crazy or bughouse. Some of the houses were moved down to the village in later years as it was too far from the center of things with no transportation. As we walked around the village especially by the P.G.E. houses we were given the once over very closely by the inhabitants as it was very small place, every one knew everyone else and most of their business also and the grapevine soon spread it around that here was the man from back east that was going to replace the existing car foreman up at the shops. The P.G.E. and Merrill & Ring logging company which operated from their office and shop in what is no known as Valleycliffe were the only employers in the village except for the service people.

At that time the ditch that is now behind the medical clinic and the Overwaitea Store ran though a flood gate through the Pemberton Road dyke, through the town under a wooden bridge near the Royal Bank, through the lane between Cleveland and Second Street behind the Chieftain Hotel, under a wooden bridge along side of the hotel and wandered through the field back of the P.G.E. houses, until it came to the dyke at the foot of Winnipeg Street.

This ditch was an old watercourse of the Squamish River and at high tides and flood conditions became quite deep. A little boy the postmaster's son Mr. Dixon was drowned in this ditch one time. On the other side of this ditch were about a dozen houses scattered over the fields up to the dyke at the west side of town.

Another wooden bridge was on Cleveland opposite Dr. Kindree's Clinic, then between the wandering ditch and the dyke back of the P.G.E. row all the way back to the dyke that ran around the shore line at the south end of town were scattered about another dozen houses. North of Pemberton Road were the groups of houses I mentioned before, then there was nothing else until you came to the Mashiter School, which was connected to town by a wooden sidewalk elevated above the perennial wet low ground.

The school was a four-room, two story wooden building, with four classrooms and a basement above ground. Past the school Cleveland curved to the right and went over the slough just in front of Daisy Barnfield's place and met the existing road just about south of the first house north of the Pentecostal Church. There was nothing else until you came to a few Indian houses and a couple of other houses just south of the shop crossing.

The road kept on going until it went through Brackendale, then went over the Checkamus River and through a hole in the wall into Paradise Valley were it ended at Levitt's farm and orchard where the North Van outdoor school is now located. Back in town Pemberton Road continued over a wooden bridge across the blind channel to Magee's dairy farm that took up all the ground now used by the Weldwood Mill. This was the village of Squamish and surrounding district when we arrived and stayed like that until people started building when lumber became so cheap in the Depression years.

On Monday after lunch I went up to the shop to meet Mr. Wilson. He came up from the boat after it came in and I was called in to the office. He was a medium sized man with light sparse hair and sharp eyes that seemed to look right through you. I can't say that I was taken to the man very much, however he asked me some more questions which I answered to the best of my ability then he turned to Mr. Kyle and said "Don't you think that he is too young to handle the job, Andy"? Andy Kyle answered," Well he has come with the best of recommendations from the C.N.R. and I think we should let him try it for awhile." I then told them that I was on holidays from the C.N.R. and I could stay about three weeks if I wrote for an extension of leave. If at that time they were not satisfied with my performance I would go back to Transcona. So with that Mr. Wilson said that it was O.K. with him as long as Mr. Kyle agreed to it. I was to start work the next morning which was July 21, 1929, After Mr. Wilson was gone Mr. Kyle took me down to the car shop and introduced me to Mr. Tom Smith the man that I was to replace. This was not a pleasant position to be in as evidently the man resented me coming and he was to go back to the tools as a carpenter in the shop working for me so I could not expect to get much cooperation from him.

There was no automobile road into the shops as I mentioned before, so the transportation for the men to the shop from the town was an old White logging truck with hard rubber tires, the back of the truck was covered with canvas with a wooden seat on each side of the truck running the full length of the back. Two men could sit up in front with the driver so the next morning I got on board this contraption in the front with Harold and away we bumped along the gravel road until we came to the clearing where we had got into Andy's car. There all the men and we got off and walked up the trail to the shop through the bush.

I talked with Harold until the whistle blew then I went down to the car shop and took up my stand by the desk in the corner. This was a dramatic moment in my life. I was only twenty-two years old and most of the men that were in the shop were a lot older than me. As the most of them were carrying on with the jobs that they were doing at the end of the week I played it cool and easy. I went around the shop told each one my name and got to know him personally. I could feel the resentment in some of them but most of them were quite agreeable and told me what type of work they were usually used to doing. As there was not a time served Carman in the whole staff I felt that I could pretty well cope with the most of them. As there was no work of any proportions going on just repair work on the wooden cars, and it wasn't train day I managed to get through the day with out any difficulties. Mary was anxiously waiting for me when I got home to see how I had made out on my first supervisory job. Of course I told her nothing to it. Little did I know what was ahead for both of us!

The next couple of weeks I played it very cool and got to know the capabilities of all the men that worked for me. There were only three of them that had served an apprenticeship and they were carpenters from shipyards in the old country. There were none with time served as railway mechanics so I figured that I could handle any questions that came up from them, which I did although once in awhile I had to stall them off until the next day so I could read up my text books at home after supper.

It was rather an awkward situation for me to be in as Tom Smith the man that I replaced went back to the tools and worked for me, as I didn't expect or get much cooperation from him. Another couple of fellows told me straight you that the job should have been theirs and I had no business taking it. I could feel the hostility against me from these men but the majority of them after a few weeks gave me their cooperation.

It might be of interesting for me to list the names of the car shop staff at the time I took over. These personnel didn't change much for a long time so their names come readily to mind. The list of the names of the men in the shop in July 1929 was made up this day of January 8, 1977.

Tom Smith, Carpenter	Louis Williams, Car Inspector
Don Fraser, Carpenter	Fred Knott, Carman's helper
Jack Edwards, Carpenter	Evo Confortin, Coach cleaner
Ed Holmes, Carpenter	Laurie Midnight, Coach cleaner
Ed Rae, Carman	Fred Cornett, Pipefitter, Tinsmith
Alex McDonald	Jim Ramsay, Lead Painter
George Kelt, Carman	Fred Barnfield, Painter apprentice

We will leave the shop affairs for a while and go back to our personal life. Squamish being such a small town as it was at the time, everyone knew everyone else and most of their business too. Mary and I were quite lonely as we hadn't had time to make any new friends and as Tom and Mrs. Smith were part of the elite of a large section of the town, mostly Conservatives, we were not invited to make their acquaintances, seeing how there was a Conservative government in power at the time. More about the local politics later. We used to take long walks after supper and as we would pass various houses we could see people peeking at us and making comments on the young couple that had come to town and taken Tom Smith's job. We spent some of our time in the evenings at Harold and Annie's house but you couldn't be there all the time. We filled in the time until the day came that we had to make up our mind if we were going to stay or go back home to Transcona as my extra leave was up the next week.

I well remember that evening. It had to be decided that night to enable us to get back in time. We walked up the road to the school on the high sidewalk and at the railroad crossing near the Overwaitea we sat on the high railing on the side walk feeling very uncertain what to do. I had sensed the feeling of the shop men by now also how some of the people in the town felt. Harold had told us to expect that as he went through the same thing the year before. You are one the other side of the fence now was his remarks and when you're the boss don't expect every one to like you. As we sat there a little black Spaniel came trotting up the sidewalk from downtown. He stopped and sniffed us and wanted to play he was such a happy little fellow that we had to oblige with a stick to chase. I said to Mary, "Well dear what do you want to do?" We had only lived in our Transcona house for six weeks, it meant leaving our house, car, new furniture, and all our relatives and friends and come to this place where we were not known, had no friends maybe some enemies already for the sake of a promotion, and an entirely new life, "She said whatever you want to do will be alright with me".

I said, "Well the little dog seems to want us to stay and I think that is the best thing for us to do". So with that decided we went back and told Harold that we would take the job and stay on.

As I said before I landed we were with the following assets. My biggest asset my young wife – without her help and comfort in the bad times this story could not be told. Forty Dollars in my pocket and a trade in my hands and head. By this time seeing that I had to work a month before I got a paycheck we were just about broke. Mary had to catch the boat the next day to go home and sell up all our belonging that we couldn't bring to Squamish, so she had to have money for the trip home. Luckily she could still use her pass.

I had to do some thing that I had never done before and that was borrowing some money. I went to Harold Bailey explained the situation to him and asked him to loan me fifty dollars. He never hesitated just asked me if that was enough and handed me the money and wouldn't take an I.O.U. So Mary was off the next day to wind up our affairs in Transcona.

Mary was gone for six weeks, during that time I had applied for a Company House in the row on Cleveland Ave and also a suite that might become vacant over McKenzie's Store. There were five suites over top of the store. Johnny Morrison and his wife Joyce lived in the largest and best one and rented out the other four. Johnny was the Manager of McKenzie's Store that was owned by Mr. McKenzie of Williams Lake. He was Johnny's Uncle and had at one time been a member of the Conservative Government in Victoria.

I had made a few friends by this time among the younger people of the town. In 1929 and 1930 there seemed to be quite a number of young people of our age who came in to the town as teachers store clerks P.G.E. employees and loggers who worked for Merrill & Ring whose camp was over in the area now known as Valleycliff. One of these young men was Art Stevenson, a real fine piano player. He used to play up at the Grouse Mountain Chalet, Vancouver Hotel, and like places. He used to hit the bottle quite heavy and I think that is the reason that he came to Squamish was to try and get away from the life he was leading in Vancouver.

When he found out that I played the banjo we got together. Another young man that we got to know was Gerry Lee. Lee came the same time as we did and was the Principal of the Mashiter School that was where the high school is now. He became a very good friend of ours and is the uncle of Dick Lazenby who is now almost one of the family. They are look alikes, think alikes, and full of ideas and energy. He used to have many deep discussions with Jerry and with his education we furthered ours in our talks.

By this time I had my banjo and Art Stevenson and I used to practice in the old Elks Hall where there was a piano. I learnt a lot from Art as he was an excellent piano player and taught me the names of various chords and how to use them. We used to play for the Saturday night dances that were held in the Brackendale Hall that was just north of the Wagon Wheel Trailer court.

There was just the two of us, Art on the Piano and me on the banjo. They were quite the bashes, all had a good time and there were very few nights that a fight didn't start outside after the bottles had been passed around a few times. You couldn't bring any liquor into a public building so they were stashed away in the various cars, buggies, or other hiding places the men had.

I have to back track a little here. Mary was away six weeks settling our affairs, we had only made two payments on the house and we still owed money on the car, so after all was done including packing up the stuff she wanted to bring to Squamish and paying her fare to Vancouver, she landed in Vancouver with $410 our total wealth. One of the suites above McKenzie's Store had become vacant, so we had to start all over again buying furniture. Some of that furniture is still around. The Toronto couch that is on the veranda at Gun Lake was our chesterfield, the two armchairs for the veranda were our two easy chairs, and the blue dining table and chairs were used until we put up the cabin at the lake. We bought all this stuff at Spencer's Department store that at that time was on the corner of Hastings and Granville, opposite the old post office.

After our belongings came from Transcona we made ourselves quite comfortable in the suite. The were two bedrooms, living room, bathroom, and kitchen with a skylight. Our fuel was coal that we got from the local dealers and was kept in four separate coal bins in the hall. This used to be a problem as they were open bins and no locks on them. Other tenants seemed to think they were common property as our bin seemed to go down awful fast, especially if one of them was out of work. We had picked up the cutest little stove for the front room. It was like a little Franklin Fireplace with doors and sat in the corner of the room and gave off a dancing light even if the doors were closed. We had no carpets on the floor just linoleum rugs. "Who cared?" only the rich people could afford carpets and we and our friends weren't in that class.

Let me describe our first Christmas away from home. Mary had bought a big chicken stuffed it and made the other goodies as we were going to have Christmas dinner alone. About four o'clock Andy Kyle came to the door and said, "#2 is on the ground at Checkamus and we have to take the wrecking crew and go right away". So with that I put on my rain clothes and away we went. There used to be a wooden bridge about a mile past the station. There is a culvert there now just at the end of those houses built on the mountainside of the tracks. #2 had been slowing down to stop at the station when the bridge collapsed under the back end of the engine and the front end of the tender. So into the water we had to go with our jacks and blocks and jack up the bridge and engine until it was level enough to get the train across. Not much of a derailment but we were all soaked through when we were finished.

I got home about 2 am on Boxing bay. When I went into the suite there was Mary with the ironing board set up in the living room ironing clothes and anything she could get her hands on with tears running down her cheeks. "What a way to spend Christmas", she said. However we had our Christmas dinner on Boxing Day.

The first winter was pretty bad for her cooped up in that little suite all day. She said she felt hemmed in with that big rock so close and felt as if she could only push it away and look across some fields she would feel better. The weather was no help either as we had a lot of alternate snow or rain that winter. Joyce Morrison who lived in the front suite looking out over Cleveland Avenue made friends with Mary and was a great deal of help to Mary in the first winter. In fact if was through Johnny and Joyce that we met many of the people in the town and they have been life long friends of ours.

For the benefit of the reader at this date January 1977 the following are the only buildings or part of them that are now left of the buildings that were the main street of Squamish at that time. The brick wall on the front of the Plaza shopping center was the front of the McKenzie's store. The Drapery store opposite Fields was Adams & Adams General Store. The Starlight Theater was the first hall in Squamish and was called the Rex Theater. The house opposite the theater belonged to the Superintendent of Merrill and Ring Logging Co. The grey house next to the Pasty Freeze and Laundry belonged to Angus McRae, father of the McRae families in the town. All the other buildings have been removed.

During that winter, I played basketball with the shop team in the Rex Theater. The baskets were set on boards in front of the stage and below the projection booth that was set further back than it is now. It was very cramped and not a full size floor. The fans used to sit up on the stage. As we had no other outside activities in the winter nearly every one who could play including two women's teams. In the men's league there were the P.G.E., Town, Elks and Loggers Teams. The games were pretty rough as the refereeing was not of the best quality. I remember one night when a quite young fellow who had been bugging me all through the game with elbow jabs in the ribs etc. suddenly found himself flying through the air and landing on the chairs on the stage. And I didn't get a game penalty for it.

The dances that were held there were real big events, with your best clothes even rented tuxedos for some of the men. Mrs. Adams used to get up ball gowns on assignment ahead of time so the ladies could have a new dress for the ball. I once made at the shop for a P.G.E. ball a revolving ball with mirrors all around it that reflected the colored light from the spotlight that gave the effect of colored snowflakes falling all around the hall. A very pretty sight.

I had promised Mary that she could go home and visit her parents the next summer, but during the winter she became pregnant with Harold. The baby was due to make his appearance in the late summer so that was the end of that. I couldn't have gone anyway as there were no paid holidays in those days, except for the supervisors or salaried men. You got two weeks holiday with pay after five years of service.

I should mention the wages paid then. Freight Carmen got 33 cents an hour; top rate carpenters and machinists got 69 cents an hour. 1 and half cents a day was taken off your pay for Workmen's Compensation. That was all the deductions. I was paid as Foreman 7 cents an hour more than the top rate so I received 76 cents an hour until I was put on a salary of $160 a month in 1933. $5 a day was the going rate for fallers and buckers in the woods. Prices for goods were much cheaper. For instance a cord of wood was $5 and I only paid the drayman for hauling our furniture from the suite to the house in the row $4 and that took the best part of half a day.

That winter the stock market drooped and the Depression started. We got daily papers from Vancouver via the Union Steamship Company but we were so isolated from the rest of the world and the majority of us didn't have any stocks anyway so that it had practically no effect on this community during the winter of 1929-30. However we would begin to feel the effects of it later on.

Cleveland Avenue – 1930 – 1934

A company cottage became vacant on the 1st of March 1930, so we moved into the little house in the row. Our house was on the opposite side of street right across from the entrance gates of where the Irly Bird Yard used to be on 37870 Cleveland Avenue.

Company house on Cleveland Avenue with Mary Stathers, her mother Mary Uhrich, Gladys Stathers, and Leona Ingraham on front steps.

There were two bedrooms, bath room, larger living room than then was in the suite, and a small kitchen on the back of the house. There was a small lean to fastened to the back part that served as an entry and a place to keep a little wood for the stoves. The yard was fenced in with a nice lawn at the front of the house and a small yard and garden in the back, there was a small shed at the back fence to store wood and coal. There were honeysuckle and climbing roses climbing up the front porch and in the summer evenings the perfume could be smelled all up the street as most of the houses had lovely flowerbeds and honeysuckle like ours.

Eric Prince Stathers with Harold Eric Stathers on his back at Cleveland Avenue.

After we had moved our stuff in and done some painting and bought the extra stuff that we needed for the house we were quite cozy there and spent many happy times visiting with our friends. We had to buy a lawn mower since we had inherited a lawn. This we bought from the hardware store, a push type brand new for $11.

During that summer I organized a softball league. I brought the first softball and bat to Squamish. They had never seen the game played and as I used to play for the Car Shop in the Transcona League I was considered a fair player. We built the first diamond on a vacant block at Third and Victoria just west of the Squamish Hotel. The hardball or baseball diamond was in the fields near the dyke at Fifth and Vancouver Streets. We organized two or three teams and played towns that would come up on the Sunday boat and play a picked Squamish team between the time the boat arrived and left.

As Harold was coming along Dr. Paul our local doctor advised Mary to see a gynecologist in Vancouver, a Dr. Bilodeau and have the baby in a Vancouver hospital when the time arrived. So he was delivered in Grace Hospital on September 17, 1930 and was a beautiful 8 pounds 4 ounces blue-eyed baby boy and I became a proud papa. There was no health insurance in those days so if you needed medical care you paid the whole shot. Just for the cost of the doctors and the hospital care, not to mention our experience of going back and forth to Vancouver on the boat cost us the equivalent of a months wages. Imagine the howl that would go up from the public if they had to pay one to two thousand dollars to have their children brought in to the world. As we worked to a budget and I have the book that we kept track of what we spent until 1933, these figures are correct and not my recollection.

By the end of 1930 we were beginning to feel the effects of the Depression. Not so much on the railway but in other ways. The loggers were being shut down for longer periods and people were hanging on to their jobs and not spending so freely. The boom was over.

During the depression the permanent residents of the town were lucky to live here. For instance, wood was readily available and close to hand as the town did not go much past Pemberton Road. People had large gardens and could preserve a lot of produce. Fish and game were easy to get and most people canned Coho Salmon and Venison. Rents were cheap. We only paid fifteen dollars a month for the Company house. Great slabs of bark used to float over from Merrill and Bing booming grounds and we used to go along the beach with the wheelbarrow and bring loads of it home. There were no log dumps as there are now on this side of the channel as Truck Logging was not used and Merrill and Ring's outfit was a railway set up that ended in a dump down past DeBeck's Mill.

I should go back to my railway life for a time so that I can keep both sides of my memoirs in line. By this time I was in to the swing of things at the shop and had learned that although I was considered a pretty smart fellow in the big Transcona plant, there was a hell of a lot that I still had to learn about running the car department on a small railroad. In Squamish we had to have the answers, there was no Montreal to go to if you were stuck as there had been on the C.N.R. I had to become familiar and partially proficient in trades that I had not been exposed to or had to learn about in Transcona. Such as pipefitting, tinsmithing, electrical work, painting steel cutting, and welding. The men didn't work on Saturday morning but the foreman and the stores had to be there so I spent my time learning and doing the different trades that I required.

I could see as soon as I got started that the Carmen were not doing all the work that they should be doing according to their trade agreement. The Boilermakers from the Roundhouse were coming down from the round house to do the steel cutting and riveting on any steel work that was required. I soon stopped that as I made up a rivet heater and borrowed the riveting gun from the roundhouse, made up some holding on tools and went to work with Alex McDonald until he was able to use the gun properly and do our own steel riveting. We had no cutting torch in the car shop so I got Andy Kyle to let me get one for ourselves which I mounted on a hand truck and after a few Saturday mornings of practice and reading up on the proper ways of using it and the dangers I was able to teach Alex and a couple of other men how to use it.

After I got that program off to a good start I started to learn how to use the electric welder. It was just in its infancy then and the heavy coated rods that are no used were not yet developed. The machines were more primitive and harder to use, however after reading some books on the subject I set up a booth in the shop and started in practicing on Saturday mornings until I could do a reasonably acceptable weld. When the coated rod came in, soon I became proficient enough to teach our apprentices how to use it. None of the other men in the shop wanted to have anything to do with it. We had to borrow the welder from the roundhouse all the time so I started up some propaganda and the round house got a new welder and we fell heir to the old one.

As we were hiring apprentices, Harold and I talked it over and decided to start an apprentice school based on the way we had been taught in Transcona. We contacted the International Correspondence School in Scranton Ohio and they agreed to send to us all the books required to get the thing going. The books on the subject that the student required were given to him with the exam taken out of the back of the book. He was given a month to complete the study of the book at home or in the class room then I took the book away from him and be wrote the exam under my eagle eye in the class room. He was given two hours a week classroom time but he had to pay for the cost of the tuition himself, as the exams were sent to Scranton to be marked.

We had to have a classroom, so I got the use of an old coach and with the help of the boys we partitioned off half of the car put in a coal stove and built desks and seats out of mostly scrap panels out of discarded coaches. This work was all done on Saturday mornings as the boys would come in without pay and work with me to get the job done so we would have some place to do the schoolwork in. Later on I got an old shack which we put across the auxiliary track east of the shop which we made in to a combined lunch room for the carman and a class room for the boys This old shack was used until the first part of the diesel shop was built, then I made the one that is upstairs in the offices. Now we had one Carman, two machinists, one boilermaker, one painter and one electrician apprentice soon after we got the school going.

Once a year I would take them to Vancouver and we would stay the weekend in a hotel and on Saturday we would visit an industrial plant that had some thing to do with railroading. This picture was taken at the C.P.R. shops at the foot of Drake Street in Vancouver.

Eric Stathers, third from left, with his first group of apprentices outside the Squamish shops (Eric Stathers).

From left: Arthur Thorne, Carman apprentice; Les Moule, Painter apprentice; Eric Stathers, Car Foreman and Apprentice Instructor; Francis McKinnon, Boilermaker apprentice; James Harley, Machinist apprentice; Bruce MacCallum, Electrician apprentice; William McAllister, Machinist apprentice.

During my half hour for lunch I would read the books that the different apprentices had to take the next month. In this way I was able to keep ahead of them so I would have the answer for them in the classroom. This gave me the opportunity to get the information required for all the trades that were needed for the operation of the Mechanical Department of the railway. This got me in to the habit of spending my lunch hour reading some technical literature even after I stopped teaching the apprentices. I didn't get any extra salary for doing this work but I got a great deal of satisfaction from doing a good thing for the boys and a great deal of information for myself.

I must say something about the political situation that existed in the town at this time. My first experience was with the painter Jim Ramsay. He may have been a good house painter but when it came to painting passenger equipment he was worse than useless. There was a sleeping car in the shop when I arrived to be painted. He was doing the interior and he had the stores buy yards and yards of linen and had spent days tacking this up around the ceiling panels so he could spray them. These panels could have been painted in half a day for each coat as they did in Transcona. I made him take this stuff down and do them by hand as the rest of the car was all real mahogany and varnished. I showed the carpenters how to make the dovetail patches that were required to repair the edges of the upper berths and windowsills and they did a good job of the work. I explained how the patches had to be stained so they were invisible and told him to try a couple before doing the whole car. I think we had to go out on a wreck, any way when I saw the job next the varnish was on and all the patches stood out like the nose on your face. I went to Andy Kyle and told that Ramsay should be fired. This he did after he had a look at the job. A few days later the shit hit the fan.

It seems that Ramey was a drinking buddy of Bob Ross the head push of the Conservative Parity in Squamish. Andy had received a call from the head office to go in to Vancouver to an investigation as to who was competent Ramsay or myself. He had time to call the C.P.R. Master mechanic in Vancouver and he said he would send up a man that could help us in the investigation.

The man that he sent up on the Sunday boat was the Painter Foreman for the C.P.R. shops in Vancouver. We met him at the boat and took him up to the shop and showed him the job and told him about the ceiling panel incident. He looked at the yards of linen that were in the paint shop and said that he agreed with us that whoever did this job did not know what he was doing. He went to the investigation with Andy and gave his opinion that was in my favour and as he was not implicated in the argument, the judgment went in my favour and the firing of Ramsay was vindicated. I breathed much easier as I had burnt many bridges behind me and had no job to go to.

The Conservative Government with Premier Tolmie was in Office then so the Conservatives were top dogs here in Squamish. The leader for the Liberal Party here was Laverne Adams of Adam and Adams General Store. Stan Clarke was the top man for the C.C.F. He ran the first gasoline pumps and parts emporium along with a coal business about were the Post Office is now.

The next run I had was when I went to get some insurance on our furniture from Bob Ross. He told me that seeing as how I worked for the government railway I should buy my coal and like supplies from him. Later on we got word from Vancouver office that we should do our grocery shopping with McKenzie's store, as John Morrison was a good Conservative too. I had never run up against this sort of thing and it didn't go down so good. The Ross crowd and the Adams bunch were at loggerheads all the time and as the Depression deepened in order to protect my job I tried to walk the top of the fence and not get too involved with either side. The policy I used for most of my life with the P.G.E.

The next person that had a great influence in my life was a man named Bill Rae. He was the Chief Boiler inspector for British Columbia and his office was in Victoria. So he was well known in government and had access to the various members of parliament. To get deeper into the political situation, Williard Kitchen and Chris Spencer were on the Board of Directors along with Tolmie and Robert Wilson was their Executive Assistant. Wilson had his informants up and down the line and also he had his own man, a Mr. Belback, who had his own speeder and traveled all over the system and reported direct to Wilson any thing that he thought he should know.

We knew what Mr. Belback's job was so we treated him politely and as far as the shop or my end of it was concerned he would always tell you if he found something that he thought was not right before he would tell Robert Wilson, he would tell us. Then if it was corrected to his satisfaction Mr. Wilson would not hear about it. So we got on fairly well with him.

Now when I went there Mr. Rae's staff the Boiler Inspectors used to come up and do the yearly inspection on the locomotive boilers, seeing as they were under the Provincial Jurisdiction. They didn't do the other railways except for the logging railroads, as the C.P.R. and C.N.R. came under the Federal Code. Before Mr. Bailey had come to the P.G.E. he had been a machinist and the apprentice inspector for the C.N.R. at the Port Mann shops. As he had spent all of his life on railroads he had a very good knowledge of locomotives and their boilers.

I can remember the arguments between the Boiler Inspectors and Andy and Harold in the office after the inspectors had put in their report and Harold or Andy didn't agree with the findings and their recommendations as to the work that had to be done on loco they had just inspected. I used to get out of the office as it didn't concern me but it got so bad that one of the inspectors refused to come to Squamish as he told Bill Rae that he had to take too much abuse from the master mechanic and loco foreman.

The Vancouver office was after us to keep our expenses down to a minimum as the Depression was coming on so Andy Kyle recommended that Harold Bailey do the loco inspection so as to save the cost of having it done by the Provincial Department. This suggestion was approved and Bill Rae's men were advised that they were no longer to go to the P.G.E. so Rae's nose was out of joint.

Now what I have to say is only my own opinion. I have no evidence to prove that Bill Rae had anything to do with it but the reader can draw his own conclusions as the story goes on. Obviously the first thing that he would have to do would be to get Andy Kyle out of the picture. Nothing was heard from him for some time and Harold and Andy seemed to think that that was the last trouble they would have with the Boiler Inspectors. By the way the inspectors used to inspect all of the rolling stock including the car equipment so I was subject to their criticisms also.

One morning a man appeared at the stores office and told Harold Thorne that he had been sent from Vancouver to be the assistant storekeeper. Thorne didn't know any thing about this so after he had it confirmed by the Vancouver office the man whose name was Davidson went to work in the stores. Art Anthony was the store clerk and took over when Thorne was away so we all were somewhat mystified. However it was soon evident what he was up to was during his noon hour he would take his lunch and walk around the shops and yards asking the men questions and seemed especially interested in the scrap bins.

One morning I was in the stores where Thorne was opening a shipment that had come in that morning. Davidson was standing by the shipping table with us as well. He picked up the invoice looked over it and said to me in front of Thorne "I wonder how much of a rake off the purchasing agent is getting from this as the cost of this is a lot higher than we paid for it on the C.P.R." I made some comment such as I didn't know as that was not part of my business, and as he was continually criticizing the P.G.E. and saying that the C.P.R. ran things a lot better than we did. We all were very careful as to what we said in his presence.

Soon after I was told that there was to be an investigation in to the workings of the Mechanical Department and Stores. It was held in Mr. Quick's office in Squamish and the man who was to conduct was Mr. Williams our Purchasing Agent from Vancouver. So on the appointed evening I went there and waited for my turn in the main office. The investigation was held in Quick's private office and one person at a time went in there. After Andy and Harold had been in and out I was sent for. Here was Davidson sitting to one side with a sheaf of papers that he would refer to as he fired the questions at us. Mr. Williams sat behind Quick's desk taking it all in while Jack Castle the Chief Clerk took it down verbatim in shorthand. He asked me some questions that I can't recall now, but it had something to do with things I had said about the C.P.R.' and the P.G.E. and then he fired what he thought was his big guns. He said, "There are dozens of brake cylinder pistons that are not worn out and you have had them thrown in the scrap pile. This is a waste of good material". I didn't answer him but turned to Mr. Williams and said, "Evidently this man doesn't know very much about the air brake system on cars. Most of these pistons he mention come off the wooden gravel hopper cars that are used in work train service.

In order to get these cars cleaned of their whole load they have to shake them, they do this by coming to an emergency stop over the place they have to dump then releasing the brakes and starting up with a jerk to shake them. Abusing the brakes this way cracks the cast iron heads of the pistons and when the brakes are set they will not hold air for very long. This could cause a run away of the whole or part of the train when working on a grade, as they are most of the time, so as we have no means to repair them we have to scrap them."

Mr. Williams said I understand that, now have you any comments to make about Mr. Davidson. I said, "Yes ever since he came here he has been criticizing the way we have to operate our small railroad in comparison with the C.P.R. He has criticized our department and also the stores as one day in Mr. Thorne's presence he asked how much rake off I thought the Purchasing Agent was getting from a shipment that had just come in, evidently trying to get me to make some remark about something that was not my business as I am not a store keeper. I told him that I didn't know and it was none of my business anyway. So with that remark I was excused.

Mr. Thorne was the next one in and he was asked if the statement I had made about the rake off was correct. He said yes as he was there too, and had heard the conversation. The investigation ended and we all went home. It wasn't very long after that that Davidson didn't come back to work. The question about the pay off must have been the sinker as Mr. Williams was always quite friendly with me any time that we met after that investigation.

However they found something that they blamed on Andy Kyle. It had some thing to do about the safety valve for a steam shovel because soon after that Andy either quit or got fired. I think he quit as he had a violent temper and he would not take to kindly to criticism even from Wilson so that was the first step towards the Inspection Department getting back into the P.G.E.

When Andy left Harold Bailey was made Master Mechanic and a man named Boomer Johnson from the machine shop was made Loco foreman. Johnson was one of the Bob Ross crowd and was promoted over younger men time served machinists who had been with the P.G.E. longer than he had. Again I don't know just how much Harold was pressured to put up with this but he didn't like or trust Johnson very much.

Now to go back to our life in the row again, I have to go back a little to the first beginnings of Squamish. In the late 1800's after other people had been here and left for various reasons. Mr. Magee a pioneer of some renown who had built his home and farm in Langley near where the fort is now, came to Squamish and preempted the land on the water front from one side of the valley to the other. Numerous channels of both the Mamquam and Squamish rivers ran through the area that is now the town. He hired a crew of Chinese who were out of work when the C.P.R was finished and with horses and manpower built dykes from Pemberton Road out to the waterfront. Some of these dykes crossed the town where the old watercourses ran. One of these dykes ran from the P.G.E. tracks and tied in with another dyke about two hundred feet south of the old steam engine in the town park.

This dyke actually separated the town in to two halves. As the cows and horses ran loose there was a well-worn trail along the top of these dykes. In some places the cows in order to get a little salt from the grass that grew along the water edge would cut a path down the dyke on to the flat where the grass grew. Some times it would be on the dykes on the upper part of the town and some times on the lower part of the town.

During the winter Equinox if there was a high tide and there happened to be high winds and gales out in the Gulf of Georgia the winds would push the water up in to the end of the sound and we would find that we were getting water in over top of the dykes. Sometimes this occurred in the upper part of the town and sometimes in the lower part.

110

Then it was all hands on deck to find the cow path that was letting the water in and with shovels and sods trying to fill the gap. If the people could get there soon enough there wouldn't be too much water get in, but if it happened in the night time or in conjunction with high water in the rivers we would have a real flood.

One day it had been raining steady all day with high winds in December and when I came home from the shop there was water all around the house and the wooden sidewalks were just beginning to float. I had supper with Mary and after supper I could see that the water was still rising. I thought that I might have to go back to the shop in case of a flood so I didn't want to leave Mary and the baby all alone in case the water started to come into the house.

I forgot to mention the reason that McGee built all these dykes. He had this large farm in Langley and wanted hay for his own stock and to sell to other people in the New Westminster area. The area where the town is now and right over to the east channel of the Squamish River produced great crops of hay. By building these dykes he kept the salt water from coming in to the fields so he could grow and harvest his crop and ship it to the Lower Mainland.

Another time that the town was flooded was during the later part of December of 1932. That year we had built at the shop a cafe car, the first dining car that the P.G.E., had ever had. This was brought on by the ever-increasing traffic to and from the Bridge River country that was just starting to boom. This was the last train down before the Christmas holidays. The train was crowded with people from the mines and up north.

That day it rained and blew all day and the night before. The gale from the south piled the water in along with a high tide and of course the inevitable happened the town was flooded, both upper and lower parts. The water was just lapping up against the floor joists in our house when the tide was at it highest so I knew that we were not going to get water in the house. The southern gale was so bad that the Union Steamship boat could not dock and had to go back to Britannia to tie up until the wind dropped. The train came in to the station and there we had about 130 passengers to look after and no place to put them.

We had to keep them in the train and feed them so whatever we had in the stores we cooked up in the cafe car. Bacon and eggs and whatever as long as it kept them going until the boat could dock. The boys in the town had a field day. They nailed pieces of wooden sidewalk together to make rafts and, charged the men in the train twenty five cents to take them over to the beer parlours in the two hotels. They kept this service up until the wee hours of the morning and made themselves more money in one night than they had made in weeks. Those kids who had got hold of a rowboat really made a killing as they could take three or four passengers to the rafts one. Finally about six o'clock in the morning the boat was able to get in and we were able to get the train down to the dock and they were away.

Nearly every fall we would have minor flooding conditions but those were the two ones I remember most of when we were living down in the row. Of course the 1940 flood was the worst the valley experienced in the memory of the people here, but that is another story that will come along in due time. Our winters seemed to be more severe than we have had over the last decade. There was no snow removal equipment available only the Public Works grader and then he had to get permission from Victoria or wherever his boss was at before the foreman could take it out. Any way we used to get these Squamish winds that would mostly blow for three days before they would blow themselves out. This particular weekend we had a Squamish wind blowing. The wind would shake the house in its gusts as if a giant had it in its hand. We had the blinds all drawn and blankets hung and tacked on the windows on the front and north side of the house to keep the wind out. As there was no insulation in the house we were cold and we spent most of our time in the kitchen by the cook stove.

There had been a snowfall of about 10 inches then it had rained on top of that then the wind got up and the whole town's streets were a sheet of ice. A knock came to the back door and there was Jerry Lee and Art Anthony. Jerry said, "Come on out Eric and try her out". "Try what out", I replied. "Take a look", said Jerry, so I put on my coat and went around the front of the house and there was an Ice Boat contraption that they had built tied up to the front fence so it wouldn't blow away. They had made it out of three old skates, some boards, and Art's wife Nina had made them a sail. So after having them in for hot cocoa off they went, they would take it back up the Pemberton Road dyke and then sail it all the way down the main street to the end of the row by what is now the Irly Bird. They along with other men kept it up for hours as long as we kept the hot drinks going in our kitchen, and I don't mean alcoholic ones.

I don't want to say too much about the winter conditions at this time as there is more to come later on, but one of the old timers who was born in the valley told me that when he was a boy he drove a team of horses across the Squamish River up by the shops hauling stove wood for the town. So it must have been colder then than it was when we came.

The next-door neighbors to the north of us were Mr. and Mrs. Baisley. He was an engineer on the line and as they had no children and Jack had appeared on the scene by now Mrs. Baisley was continually doing things for Mary and the kids. They were very fine people and we liked them very much although they were quite a bit older than we were. Further down the row lived another Engineer and his wife Mr. and Mrs. Mike Powell. They also had no children but we did not know them only to say hello too. Mike had the night run of the mixed out of Lillooet, as he wanted to take some time off.

This is another story but that night they had real bad weather conditions in the north, and the engine that Minor was driving went through the Fountain Bridge, fourteen miles north of Lillooet and he was killed along with two other men from Squamish. This was a big blow to the people here to have three of there men killed at the same time and all on the railroad. We went up then with the Auxiliary but all we could do was to get the tender off the locomotive and tie it down so it wouldn't roll in to the Fraser Canyon as we didn't have the heavy equipment required to get the engine and tender back up on the tracks. So we came home and the Engineering Department was able to build up the bridge and get the road going while the engine lay along side of the bridge.

Now again I am going to show how the Ross crowd were trying to get my job back for one of their own. I was called in to the office soon after we got back and Andy Kyle said to me, "Eric, have you been talking to any one as to how that engine should be taken out of Fountain?" Not that I can recollect except to you and Harold Bailey, as I haven't much of an idea on how you go about it.   "Well I have just had a phone call from Mr. Wilson and he says that you are going around town saying that if the engine doesn't come out your way you will see that it doesn't come out but goes down in to the canyon instead. Now if you have said that and mean it Eric, I have to give you your discharge immediately" So what am I going to tell him?

I said, "Andy that's a G.D. lie. I told you when you hired me that I had no wrecking experience. And when you and I stood on the gaping end of that bridge and looked down at that engine laying there I thought to myself how in the world does one go about getting this engine back up on to the tracks. I have never made that statement and I haven't the foggiest idea as how to go about getting it back up again. I would like to meet the man who made that statement to Mr. Wilson and I'll cram his lying words down his throat". Mr. Kyle said, "Thanks. Eric I'll tell Mr. Wilson just what you said". I never heard any more of that episode but I had to very careful as to what I said about the railroad and I never fraternized with any of the men who worked for me in the car department.

One of these men that were spying for the Ross crowd was a Carman named Andy Mahood. He was a car inspector also and I knew that he was passing on all the tidbits that he could get to Ross and they would be relayed on. So in order to protect myself if there came to be an investigation as to my competence, I kept a close watch on Mahood and his work. I still have in my possession the note book I kept where I recorded all the things that Andy Mahood did wrong in his work and he wasn't so hot at it either so that I would be able to show in my defense if needed that the information came from a man that was not able to do his own job properly and I could quote dates, time, and the things that he had either missed or did wrong. I never had to use this info but for some reason or other it laid around my desk all those years and I still have it.

Now to go along further in the political shenanigans that were being played at that time, Laverne Adams was the head of the basketball organization and some how or another Bob Ross got hold of the agency for renting the Rex Theatre. Soon after he got the agency he raised the rent on the Rex to such an extent that even if we increased our yearly dues we would be broke or possibly unable to finish the winter season that was just about to begin. Laverne called a general meeting of the basketball club in the dining room of the Squamish

Hotel to discuss the situation. Now you could become a voting member of the club by buying a membership ticket for $1; if you played you had to pay more. These tickets were sold to the general public to help finance the club and they enabled the buyer to see all the local games free.

As soon as Ross heard of this meeting he and his cronies, of which Boomer Johnson was one, were out selling and buying tickets for their own crowd so they could pack the meeting. I well remember that night. There were so many in attendance that we all could not get in to the dining room and the people overflowed in to the lobby. Laverne explained the situation to the crowd and put the question. So we play until we have spent all our money on rent and maybe not finish the season, or do we not play at all and maybe if we hang on to what we have we can use it to start a place to play in the future? The Ross crowed of course voted to spend the money and play, but the majority said "No", so there was no basketball that winter at all.

This aroused the anger of other citizens of the town who had no affiliation with either party or who where mostly P.G.E. men who had children coming up who would be deprived of any active sport in the Rex. So they got together and decided to build a hall. This would be built owned and controlled by the P.G.E. Employees Association and would not have any thing to do with either political party. A meeting was called and the basketball association was asked if they would make a substantial contribution towards this hall from their funds. This they agreed to and we were off to a flying start. Money was raised by all means. A great deal of money was raised by a monthly raffle on shares of the various gold mines that were very popular then such as Bralorne, Minto, and others in the Bridge River country. The P.G.E. was very good. They obtained the three lots that we needed, gave us used bridge timbers for the heavy foundations that were required, lent us their big cement mixer, gave us cement at cost, and many other thing that were required as the building progressed.

The hall was all put up by voluntary labour except for the wages of Frank Scott who was in charge of construction. All employees were asked to give at least one week's work in labour or one week's wages. That is those who lived in Squamish. Nearly every one came through, and many of us gave not a week but weeks and weeks of labour, especially those from the mechanical department. By the end of the summer the building was up with the four walls standing the inside partitions and the outside buttresses up but no roof on it. The roof was constructed from huge trusses designed like a bridge and using oil bridge truss castings for assembly. They had been built on the ground and some of them were ready to put up.

Before they could be put up, a derrick pole had to be put up in the middle of the floor, so we said to Frank Scott hold off a while we have worked hard all summer we are going to have an open-air dance before you clutter up the floor. So we had this dance one Saturday night, I well remember it. The ladies had made and were continually making coffee,

114

hot dogs were cooking along with hamburgers, and as it was quite cool you had to keep either dancing or eating to keep warm. There was a brilliant moon shining down in to the interior of the building which gave ample lighting for those who wanted it and shadows for the more romantically inclined, which added to the pleasure of having a wonderful time after working so hard on the project. Truly a night to remember all your lives and on top of that we made some more money from the dance for the kitty.

That winter we had it good enough to play basketball on the floor that was laid out so that we had a full size basketball floor with lots of room for throw-ins. Three badminton courts were laid out across the floor. There was a balcony around three sides of the hall, a dining room and kitchen on the second floor which was used for smaller doo's and meetings, then on top of that was a suite for the caretaker. It was a beautiful hall when we got it finally finished and was a credit to the town as this was built by the people themselves, no grants or gifts from the government such as there is now. I was President of the association for about three years and was on the committee for many years. I used to be the M.C. or Master of Ceremonies at the dances and had to announce the next dance and keep order on the floor in case of any trouble with drunks. One dance the hall was so full with people from Woodfiber and Britannia who had come over for this big dance that, the floor was just a jumping.

I didn't notice it, but the stage folded up in to the wall for the games and we let it down for the dances so it wasn't anchored to the floor, and the stage was bouncing out the floor along with the orchestra that the piano was gradually creeping over to the edge of the stage. All at once there was a huge crash and I looked behind me and there was the piano player sitting on his bench with his hand in the air but no piano, we had danced the piano right off the stage. BANG, Well with about six husky men we picked up the piano and put it back on the stage in front of the player, he walloped a few chords proclaimed it O.K. and I hollered for the dance to proceed. Lots of fun and no people killed.

Just one more thing to say about Bob Ross. He had been such a miserable old S.O.B. that he made the rest of us get off our butts and build a hall to use for the benefit of the whole town. Before the new school was built with the big gym, the school board used to bus the pupils down to the hall in the winter for their gym periods. We used to get revenue from this to keep the hall going. It was always a financial battle to keep the hall going. We received no help from the town we even had to pay taxes. Imagine what the golf course would wind up as if the town charged them taxes. So after the new school was built there was less and less use for the big hall. There was less demand for big dances and it was too big for smaller events. Basketball was being played in the school gym so eventually a buyer was found for it and sold for a few thousand dollars. This money was turned over to start the student scholarship fund that is awarded every year in school. This building is opposite the bowling alley and is now converted in to the apartment block known as Hudson House.

At this time about 1932 the Depression deepened and many men were out or work, as there were no jobs to he found. The Provincial Government started to build relief camps for the single men that were out of work. At Darrell Bay where the ferry comes in there used to be an old brick works. There were some old buildings there that were in pretty bad shape that were used at times by the odd boat that would tie up there in a storm or men passing through. If you went down between the P.G.E. tracks and the shore no doubt you would still find some of the broken red bricks from the plant. In 1932 the government took this place over and rebuilt the old buildings and added some more and had a camp that held about two hundred and fifty single men.

Among these men were lawyers, engineers, and all classes of tradesmen and labourers. They were given their board and room and twenty-five cents a day spending money for tobacco and other essentials. For this they had to work on the proposed road between Squamish and Britannia, They did this work with pick and shovels and started in the gravel sections as there was no money to spend on dynamite for the rock work. They leveled out a flat section with wheelbarrows where the road was to go. This is how the road was started behind the camp, more of a make work program to keep the men occupied.

The camp had a boat and a small scow that they used to come to town for supplies and to transport men. When the men received their small pay they used to come over to the town on a Saturday night and most of them would try and drown their sorrows in the beer parlour. They used to troop past our house on the row and back again after the beer parlour was closed. They would create quite a disturbance stumbling in and out of the ditches and singing and shouting as they went by. Not all of these men were like that, really I suppose it was the minority as some of these men stayed in Squamish and became solid citizens in later years.

They used to come to the dances in the big hall and try and sneak in without paying their way. You could hardly blame them, as they didn't have the money or the good clothes to attend like those of us who were working. I well remember one night of these dances when an argument started between one of them and Pete Rebegliati who was the road master for the railway in this area. He was a tough hardy man who feared neither man nor beast. He found one of these relief camp lads in the hall and forcibly ejected him. Now knowing Pete quite well I don't suppose that he was too gentle in the manner in which he put the fellow out. As there was a bunch of the relief camp men outside of the hall listening to the music, they reacted to one of their group been thrown out rather violently.

One of the men called Pete a dirty name and Pete started after him. Now Pete fought rough and tumble and if had ever got his hands on this young man who was much smaller than him he would have crushed him flat. But, unbeknown to Pete, or us this man was an ex-prize fighter and he carefully kept out of Pete's reach and proceeded to cut him to ribbons with his fast footwork and jabs to the face and belly. It was something to watch as he demolished a man much larger and stronger than himself. Finally Pete was like an old bull in the ring with blood running down his face and chest, but he wouldn't quit, so a bunch of us jumped down the steps and there was enough of us to put the relief camp men out of the way and we dragged Pate back in to the hall, washed off his face and took him to the Squamish Hotel were he was staying over night. He came in to the shop the next day and he was talking to Harold and I and others about the previous evening out of his swollen eyes and cut face, he said, "That's my last fight, I am to old now to act like I used to, last night proved it". I don't think Pete ever had another fight after that night.

During the winter of 1934-35 we had real heavy snow conditions, more about this later, however we had a good four feet of heavy wet snow on the roof of the car shop and it kept, on raining and freezing. We were becoming alarmed about the heavy load on the car shop roof. The Chief Engineer Mr. Bates had me set up a rod on to the trusses hanging down to a fixed point so I could measure the deflection of the roof trusses. This I did and had to report every hour as to how much the roof was sagging. He decided that he had to get help so the next morning there was a large group of these relief camp men brought to the shop and put up on the roof to cut channels through the snow to let the water run off and relieve the load.

These men were paid twenty-seven cents an hour for doing this work and as it was still raining and they didn't have proper clothing. It wasn't long before they were soaked. They came in to the car shop at noon and grouped around the two coal stoves that were our only heat and tried to get warm and dried out a little. I saw some of them take out their sandwiches out of their pockets and they were soggy and a crumpled mess. However that was all they had to eat so down it went. It was a most pitiful sight to see what these men went through to earn a few dollars for extra spending money. Some of them didn't make it through the afternoon, as their backs couldn't take it. The next day only about half of them showed up for work but those who did were kept on for a few days more to help the section men catch up to all the extra work the heavy snow made.

Those were the conditions that the single men had to put up with during the Depression. For the married men they would get the dole and some clothing for the kids, just a bare sustenance, that's all.

My family has said to me, "Why did you stay with the P.G.E. and take all that guff from the management and the Ross Group?" Well this is why. Here I was with my wife and family with no one to turn to and if I hadn't hung on to my job I would have been turned out of the company's house and how would I have taken care of the family. That is why I am trying to show how the Depression had such an effect on the lives of those who went through even if they had a job. If you had a job you had to help those in the family who didn't which we had to do also.

In late 1931 Mary again became pregnant, due to the problems she was having with her health since Harold was born our local doctor sent her to a specialist in Vancouver a Dr. Burnwell. This meant more expense which we could ill afford at this time. However we struggled along and in July 15 1932 Mary presented me with our second son. We named him Jack Kenneth Stathers. Where the Kenneth came from I do not recall, as there is no Kenneth in our family names that I know of. He was born in St. Paul's Hospital and I well remember the day that I took them both out to bring them home. At the checkout where you had to settle your bill was an old battle-axe of a nun. She wanted me to pay the full cost of the stay in the hospital and I didn't have the money to pay the whole thing. I tried to reason with her and said that I could pay it off at ten dollars a month. This wasn't good enough for her and she told me that we had no business having babies if we couldn't pay to bring them in to the world. Well! This made me quite angry and I told that old shrew that if she was a man I would have wrapped the desk around her head and that was how I was going to pay the bill and that I was going to take my wife and child home.

At the same time I had to pay for a home help to look after Harold and to help Mary in the house, also there were her expenses while she was staying in Vancouver and the costs of the trips to town. Also my brother Tom had got laid off from his job in Transcona after 14 years of service. I was sending what money we could spare to him each month and paying ten dollars a month to Dr. Burwell so we were skating on pretty thin ice financially. However how tough it had been on Mary washing diapers in the bath tub with a scrubbing board we did the big thing and bought an electric washing machine from the Squamish Hardware and they let us pay for it at $5.75 a month. This was the first thing that we had ever bought for the home on credit and it was a godsend with those two young children in the house.

One day we very nearly lost Jack. He was just two months old and laying in the baby carriage. The peas were ripe in the garden and Harold had got hold of a pea pod and wanting to share it with his brother he popped a green pea in the baby's mouth. Luckily Mary came in the room in time and saw the baby going blue in the face. She yelled for me as I was home between us both with me holding the kid in the air by its feet we managed to dislodge it.

Now early in 1932 Jack Castle, the Chief Clerk here, Harold Bailey, and a couple of others got Bob Wilson to subdivide the area now known as Wilson Crescent from Cleveland Avenue up to Buckley's Crossing into parcels of land of an acre and a half, more or less. Castle took the first one and Harold Bailey the second one on the corner of Wilson Crescent and Cleveland Avenue. Now, even with the tough times we had a few dollars, so knowing that if I lost my job I would be turned out of the company's house and thinking that even if we only had a shack on the lot, what with fish in the river of which there were plenty in those days, deer to be had in season, and a big garden with some chickens we wouldn't starve. After talking it over with Mary, we put our name in for a lot also. We go the next one in on Wilson Crescent and the telegraph operator, Ernie Reeves, got the one opposite Harold on the other side of the street. Now this was all bush and big stumps left over from early logging operations, right from Castle's Crossing up to the next railroad crossing except for Barnfield's house where it is now next to the Tantalus Apartments. I will never forget the Sunday morning when Harold, Ernie, and I went up to the lot and tried to figure out just who was whose.

As the lots were not yet surveyed, Harold had a map from the Engineering Department showing the placement of the lots. We paced off the required length from Castle's Corner and said "Well, Harold that must be yours to the left. Ernie that must be yours to the right and I am in about one hundred and eighty feet. So with that we spit on our hand and tried to cut down trees and bush. I started to clear a trail in to what I thought was the corner of my property. It wasn't until some months later when the land surveyors came that we had cleared off the road as well as our own pieces.

Now there were no bulldozers in the valley then, so clearing of land was done with either blasting the stumps, pulling them out with a winch and cables or using a horse instead of the winch. All of these methods required a lot of chopping roots and digging around the big stumps. I had a fifteen-foot length of five inch tubing that was quite heavy, but once you got this under a root and chinned yourself on the other end you could move a lot of root. Power saws were unknown then so it was either the buck saw or a big cross cut saw with two handles on it that we had to use to fall trees and cut up the wood. I took nine cords of wood off the portion that we cleared to build our house. Mary got quite a few blisters on her hand from being on the other end of the crosscut saw.

Our lot was one and one third acres. We paid ten dollars down and ten dollars a month until two hundred and twenty dollars had been paid. This was the total cost of the lot, except for the survey, which only cost the three of us twenty-five apiece as we went in together on the survey. Now this doesn't seem much money these days, but then it was quite a lot for un-cleared land.

Now I got a case of stumping powder and I got a man to blast the stumps. He was quite good at this and didn't put too big a charge under the stumps so as to not blast away all the topsoil. After he had gone around the lot, blasting most of the alder stumps, I along with Harold used to hire a horse off Mr. McGee to pull out the loosened stumps. Now this beast was an old hand at this game and he knew just how to go about it. We would rig up the cables and blocks on the stump, then hitch the horse up to the end of the cables. Now we called the horse Farting Jenny, because after we had hitched him up we would holler at him to get going. No way. He would turn his head around look the situation over then usually let off big blast then take off on the dead run until he was either stopped with the pull on the cable or the stump would be out.

When we had a quantity of stumps pulled out we had to get rid of them so I picked out a big alder tree off to one side of the lot, climbed up it and hung a block on the top of it and ran a long cable through it. I would hitch up old Jenny to the end of the cable and the other end to the stump and then away she would go until the stump was the top of the tree, and then back her up until the stump was on the top of the pile. I had a pile about twelve feet high that the next fall and winter we burnt up.

119

That old horse I think new more about clearing land than the whole bunch of us put together. It was hard work and we got lots of blisters and aching backs but it was a challenge to us and we were working towards building our own home. We kept at it. Jack was in the baby carriage by this time, so on Sundays Mary would pack a lunch, Harold would get on his trike, and we would take off from the row and make a picnic out of the day. We had no car and no money either so this was the way we spent the summer and fall of 1932.

I remember one day that summer, I was going to fall a big alder tree so I told Mary to take the boys and herself away from the direction of which the tree was going to fall which she did. I had the tree just about ready to fall when a strong gust of wind came up from the south and the tree started to fall toward the family. Mary let out a yell to warn me and I saw what was about to happen so I made a mad dash towards them scooped up Harold in one arm and with the other pushed the baby carriage ahead of me. The tree came down just behind me, the top part of the tree brushed my back, and some of the branches stuck the carriage the kids started to howl and we were all shaken up by our close call but no one was hurt.

That some summer a man named Cliff Thorne offered to blast the stumps for me, as I didn't know how to use dynamite. This he did. We would set up two or three stumps to blow with a long enough fuse to let us got over to the Mashiter School, and then we would sit on the fence rail and wait for them to go off. We would each count out loud the number of explosions then wait for ten minutes for the smoke to clear away then go back and set up some more to blow out. If you want back too soon and breathed too much of the powder fumes you would get a powder headache that was most painful he told me.

This time we had set up six stumps to go off, as this was all the powder we had left, but Cliff knew enough about this game to keep one stick case of a misfire that up to then we hadn't had. So there we sat on the fence counting the blasts. On. Two. Three. The big one that had ten sticks under it Boom Four. A little one Five, then we waited, and waited no Boom. Cliff said, "Well I guess we have a dud, what was your count"? "Five".

I replied. "We will wait another twenty minutes then if it doesn't blow we will go and take a look", with that we waited out the time and then we went back and surveyed the results. There it sat a double stump with seven sticks of powder under it just as we had left it. "What do we do now I asked?" Cliff said, "You dig down the hole and carefully scrape the dirt out until you feel the end of the sticks, be careful and don't go past the sticks as you may hit the cap and it might blow." I said, "Who me?" Cliff said, "Yea, I'll get this last stick ready so we can set off the stuff that didn't blow."

Now may be I am chicken and an old Powder Man would laugh at this but I don't mind admitting that I was damn scared. However I had to do what he said if I wanted the stumps out so I very carefully started to scratch away at the dirt where the dynamite was buried following the burnt fuse down. I kept wondering how many pieces of me would be found around the lot if it went off while I was digging. Other pleasant thoughts were crossing my mind as I worked, such as how would if look without a head. However I finally felt the end of the bundle of sticks, carefully scraped away the dirt, and the whole end was exposed, then Cliff took over. He popped the one stick in along with the other seven, packed the hole tight with dirt and lit the fuse. We took off to the school fence and waited. It wasn't long until it went off. That was the end of the blasting and I was glad it was over.

All that winter of 1932-33 we were looking at house plans and trying to figure out just what we could afford to build. I had my draughting gear so with that and borrowing ideas out of books I drew up a plan of what we were going to build. Now we were in the depths of the Depression by then and many lumber mills were closed down, but those people that had a little money could get lumber very cheap from a mill that was still operating up at Parkhurst. The Keely Lumber Company owned it the forerunner of Empire Mills that was taken over by Weldwood, the company that now operates the big mill here.

Harold Bailey was getting ready to build his house at the same time, so we put our orders together and got a carload of lumber from the Parkhurst Mill. When it came down, as there were no trains on Sundays in those days, we had it spotted back of our houses on the main line and we just dumped it off behind the place where each house was going to be. As Harold could run an engine and was the Locomotive foreman, he had an engine from the shop and moved the car, as we wanted it, then took it out of the way when we were finished.

Now lumber was cheaper than concrete so we both ordered forty foot cedar timbers six inches thick and twelve inches wide for each house for the foundations we used six by eight solid fir timber for posts and floor beams and by the time we had them all in place I tell you those foundations were strong enough to hold up a three story house. As we had the cash saved up it was a cash deal with the mill, and as cash was hard to come by we got a pretty good deal. For those big forty foot timbers we only paid ten dollars a thousand, for the beams and all the framing lumber such as two by fours, two by sixes we also paid only ten dollars a thousand. For the clear one by six beveled cedar siding fifteen dollars and for the one by four clear air-dried flooring twenty-five dollars a thousand. A lot of the lumber was clear and I made a lot of the trim out of the clear boards.

Now the whole order of lumber for the house came to about two hundred and fifty dollars. We didn't' have much more than that in the bank so by the time we had paid the bill we were just about broke again. So we pulled the lumber up on the lot, stacked it all so it would dry, and then started to get the place ready on the lot for the house. Now though I had served an Apprenticeship, could use the tools, and had taken up Architectural Draughting in Apprentice School, what I didn't know about the actual work of building a house would have filled a few books. With the help of Mr. Scott, our bridge and building Master on the railway who told us how to go about siting up to get the foundation level and square, I got the foundations built and the shiplap for setting the floor on. This was in the late summer and fall of 1933. It then started in to rain and my floor started to swell and pull the posts out of square. I was getting pretty worried, as I couldn't work fast enough part time to get the frame up and the roof on. Then one day along came a man called Dawson, his children and descendants still live in Squamish today.

Budget for the construction of Eric and Mary's Wilson Crescent home.

He went to Harold and made a deal with him then came to me and wanted to build my house too. Well as we were broke I told him that I just couldn't afford to spend much money on the building however when he offered to put up the frame roof, put on the shingles, frame the inside, partitions and put the shiplap on the outside of the house for seventy five dollars I told him to go ahead and I would pay him as soon as I could. So this he did with Harold's house and then ours. By late fall and before the winter rains came our house was up to that extent with no windows or doors in it. Just to mention this Herb Dawson went over to the relief camp and picked up a bunch of fellows, Lord knows what he

122

paid them, and they actually did the work on the two houses while Dawson did the bossing. He was a fairly good carpenter so I had no complaints with the job they did.

Wilson Crescent – 1934 -

I then started to work on the inside nearly every night and Saturday afternoon and Sundays I would be up at the house. We quit work at four thirty or so and at six o'clock every night I would leave the house on the row and go up to the house and work until ten. I kept this up all the winter of 1933-34 and by the 13th June 1934 we moved in. Now there was only shiplap on the outside and shiplap on the inside. The plumbing was in and the floor finished and enough of the kitchen cupboards up so Mary could feed us. You could say it was just habitable. However we had got away from paying that monthly rent so now we could spend that money on more building materials for the house.

Now we could start working on the house both on the outside and the inside so in the good weather we worked on the outside and in the winter we worked on the inside. We had the upstairs floored over with shiplap so I put up a workbench up there and I started on the cupboards for the kitchen and bathroom. Now I couldn't afford to buy plywood, as it was very dear and scarce then so we used to get materials at the stores department at the shops in tea chests that originally came from India. I had Harold Thorne save me these tea chests as they were made from thin plywood held together with metal corners. I took these tea chests apart for my plywood then I made all the frames from the flooring that I had left over. I mortised and tenoned the frames by hand and used the plywood for the panels and in this way made all the cupboard doors for the whole house with out any machinery at all.

The counter and the cupboards in the cottage at Gun Lake are the original cupboards or I should, say what is left of the ones that I built by hand for the house on Wilson Crescent. Now to explain a little about the method of house building used in the sticks in those days. Lumber was cheap. Gyproc was expensive, as it had to be crated and shipped by Union Steamship to Squamish, so we only put Gyproc in the kitchen, dining room, and the living room ceilings. As the shiplap had been put on the rest of the house in 1933, by the winter of 1934 it had been pretty well dried out.

Now usually people would put over the shiplap felt paper. This was a very heavy grey paper that came in 36-inch widths. It was about as thick as 50 pound roofing paper today but much softer. The method of applying was to paste the wall then paste the felt and slap it on the walls and ceilings. The joints were butted together and if you pushed the joints hard together you would raise the joint which when dry could be sand papered down so you could hardly see the joints, especially if wall paper was applied over the felt. The one fault with this method was that if the shiplap was not even you could see the joints of the boards.

So I didn't want to have a cheap looking job so during that winter of 1934-35 I set every nail in the shiplap in every room of the house. Then I started in and I planed by hand every shiplap joint in the whole place except for the ceilings where the Gyproc was going. We did a careful job of putting on the felt paper and after the paint or paper was applied over top, you could not see a joint anywhere. The walls looked as if they were plastered. I would venture to say that even after all these years; you would have a hard time to tell how it was built on the inside.

Well we kept plugging away at it and it was some time in the fall of 1937 that we had got all the lawns in, the fences up, and we had just finished the last lick of paint on the outside of the house. The inside was also finished. We had taken the curtain rods off and put them back five times before we had finally got the inside to our liking. It was a lovely summer evening and it was just getting dusk. I had put away the paintbrushes and said to Mary, "Well there it is dear, after five years of working it is finally finished, come out and take a look." We went out on the road and the house just glistened in its new coat of oil paint. It was a feeling that you have to experience to understand it was all ours, not a penny owing on it and we had our own home at last. Mary said to me, "Now I know how God felt on the seventh day".

Wilson Crescent home finished Labor Day 1937 with Mary Stathers, Eric Stathers, and Leona Ingraham standing in front.

The cottage on Wilson Crescent that I built next door for my parents with my father William and William King on top step with mother Mary with sister Sally seated below.

My parents lived in the house next door for twelve years for about $600. I had spent, a year of my life's spare time building it and supplied the lot thinking that they had been well treated. This my father couldn't see as in his mind as sons were supposed to contribute to the family and be subordinate to the dictates of the father. However we settled it by saying that we would split the rent fifty: fifty and I sent their part in to them. The rest of the family (and I speak of those that are gone, not my own) took their side and I was told in no uncertain terms by my Aunt and my own brother what they thought of me, and how I was cheating my own mother and father out of what was rightfully theirs. As by this time our own boys had grown to the point that they were getting near the end of their schooling here and had said that they wanted to go to college, it meant that we had to keep on scratching to enable the boys to get an education they wanted and we would need every penny we could save to do it. Further unpleasantness transpired as time went on and they got old, however, it has no bearing on this story and will not interest the reader. I will wind this part up with this thought that when the last days came of all those who criticized me, who did they turn to? Me. I had to take the burden of the last rights and the settling up of the estates of all except my Uncle Will King who I think was on my side but had to keep quiet as his wife was so down on me. I will leave the reader to be his own judge of who was right or wrong.

Left: Father William Stork, wife Mary with Aunt Sally and William King at house next door.
Right: Eric Stathers, Uncle Will, and brother Bill during time that my parents lived next door.

Now I don't want to give the impression that all we did was work. I had taken four years of First Aid in Tranacona and a couple of years after we came I started to take it again under our town doctor Dr. Paul. He was the exact copy of the old country doctor, who would come out at any time of the day or night and minister to his flock. He never kept track of what people owed him and every so often you would give him ten dollars or so and say "put it toward my account please". It would go in to his pocket and you never got a receipt or a bill. At least that was my experience. He had been all through the First World War as a doctor and had a lot of experience. He didn't fool around whenever there was an accident he went right to work on the patient, a lot of time without local anesthetics. He put seven stitches in my head once without any pain killer, no messing around, just shaved the head and went to work with the needle and thread.

He wanted me to take my Instructors exam, so he would start a class then let me take over, pop in once in awhile to see how I was doing and I would carry on. After that I took over the first aid classes that we had every winter.

By this time Hitler was starting to raise a ruckus in Europe, people were beginning to think that all might not be rosy. This may have had some effect on the people taking the classes, however I enjoyed giving them and made friends with many people that last to this day. We also had the basketball and badminton in the big hall with games away to Britannia

126

and Woodfibre, our dances and the sports days of the 24th of May and the 1st of July that the Elks put on a big day for the kids in the town.

As I was an Elk by this time I was quite active in this organization. On top of that there were the dances and we used to have our Saturday card parties with our friends. No alcoholic drinks were served at these get-togethers as there is now, it just wasn't done and any way liquor was hard to get as it had to come in from Vancouver or Lillooet and we couldn't afford to buy it any way, except for Christmas or New Year.

We worked hard and played hard at our different doings. By this time we had the chickens going well, a big garden and there were lots of fish in the river that we often got, more about our hunting and fishing trips later. We got grouse, ducks, and deer in season that we used to can with a canning machine. The boys had their chores to do and had to help with the chickens and the garden so it was a family affair and many a meal we sat down to were there was not something or maybe the majority of the food on the table raised on our place or had come from the wild game or the river.

I spent many hours with the boys, showing them the right way to do things. When we built the chicken house, Jack made out the bill of materials. He was only nine or ten at the time and he went over to the mill and put in the order. I showed them how to cut the rafters and the window frames and they practically built the chicken house on their own with me helping them. Many a time I could have done the job in half the time myself but I would show them how to do it and work along with them until it was done. In this way they were part of the family and could take credit for a lot of the work that was done around the place and while they were doing this they were learning how to use the tools. Mind you they didn't always take kindly to having to do some of the things that were set for them to do when other kids were out playing, but it has paid off in the long run and as young men have taken on jobs and done them successfully for which I take a small part of the credit for with the way I made them stick with anything we tackled.

***

Some two years have gone by since I put the last lines on the forgoing part of this book. Since that time, with the urging of Dick Lazenby and the desire on my part, with his help I have put together a fifteen-chapter manuscript of my life as a wrecking foreman that was part of my duties in my work with the P.G.E. This is now finished so I now can get back to doing some more on this work.

Today is Jan 22 1981. Where to start? I must take the reader back some years, as I wanted to finish describing how we built the two houses on Wilson Crescent. In 1931 the big Depression was in its depth. We had received directions from Vancouver Office that we had to cut our shop cost away down. When it was put up to a vote of the men in the shop to chose short time or layoff's the men voted for short time, so the men were only working three or four days a week. The foreman worked five and a half days but we took a 10% cut in wages. We did every thing we could to keep material costs down, reusing scrap material, cutting damaged bolts down to make shorter ones, and so on.

I learned of this story of what was happening up the line at the mining district of what is now known as Bralorne at the same time as we were struggling to keep the P.G.E. going. I think it quite interesting and worth telling.

In 1924 Mr. David Sloan who owned a half interest in the old Pioneer mine hired a Mr. Bob Ekloff to take a crew of men into the mine and start working it. Mr. Ekloff in later years became a good friend of mine so I know this story is true. He and his crew started the Pioneer Mine and stayed with it until it was closed down and amalgamated with Bralorne. In the fall of the year 1931 they had received their grub supplies for the winter and were expecting to stay there as usual. However Bob got a phone call from Mr.Sloan that there was no money left in the kitty to pay the men's wages and that he was to tell the men this and that they had better get out of there before they got snowed in for the winter. This was indeed bad news as jobs were very scarce in Vancouver and mines were shutting down all over the Province.

Bob went to his wife Ina and told her the bad news. How are we fixed for food supplies he wanted to know, as when the winter set in they were often snowed in for weeks as that is heavy snow country and there was no snow clearing equipment to work on the road from Shalalth. Every thing had to come in by sleigh and horses in the wintertime. "Well Bob", she said. "What with the preserves I have put up and the vegetables in the root cellar, if you can bring in the odd deer or two why I am sure we wont starve until they can get to us in the spring. With that assurance Bob rounded the men of the crew in the bunkhouse and told them the news. "There is no money to pay your wages. You have enough grub in the cookhouse to keep us going until spring providing we get some deer and maybe a moose and fish out of Gun Lake. So what do you want to do, go now or stay and work the mine" "What are you going to do Bob", was the question put to him. "My wife and I are going to stay, even if you all pull out", was the answer. "We will take a vote and let you know in an hour", they said so as the vote was to stay the crew stayed on and they got a team of horses and pulled a stamp mill down from another old mine that was abandoned that Bob knew about set it up and worked all winter getting out ore, crushing it, and getting ready to pour a gold brick in the spring. This they could do as they had already got the machinery up to do this.

In April 1932 Bob put a call in to Mr. Sloan and told him to get up to the mine as soon as he could. Sloan caught the next train up to Shalalth and when he arrived at the mine Bob said, "Come with me I want to show you something", with that he took him down to the place where they poured the molten gold in to molds and there was a small gold brick about half the size of a standard gold brick. "Give me that", said "Sloan. ""I am getting to Vancouver as soon as I can and when I show this around the Stock Exchange I will be able to raise enough money to keep this mine going". So he took off and soon the money came up so Bob could pay the men their wages and they all kept on working. Bob didn't get his salary until sometime later but this started the second round of mining fever in the Bridge River Valley which due to the guts of Bob and his men was the start of better times for us all.

When I told him what I had been doing to keep the car department going at the same time as he was doing his thing up there, he said, "Guess you and I helped to get this part of B.C. going again in those tough times. Maybe we should apply for a medal", with jocularity, of course.

Then as the demands of the mining boom required better service than we could give with our old worn out passenger equipment we started to improve our service. First we built a combination dining and chair car from one of the old steel trailer coaches that came from the North Shore line that closed down in 1928 and had been lying around the shop. The Oregon Electric Railway running out of Portland had closed down and they had a lot of wooden suburban coaches and baggage cars for sale. Mr. Bailey went to Portland and bought same of this equipment and we started to convert it to as near standard equipment as we could. This put the men in the shop back to work full time again when many other parts of the province were still feeling the Depression as bad as before.

As the mine demands increased, so did our workload in the shop. We built baggage cars, two more dining cars and open top observation cars from either the North Shore stuff or the Oregon equipment all with the limited tools and materials we had to work with. True, looking back now it was pretty crude passenger equipment compared to the C.P.R. or C.N.R. equipment but we had very little money to work with and a great deal of ingenuity was needed on my part and the men of the car department to turn out what we did.

This was the turning point in our lives in the shop and as the years rolled on many other demands were made on us to keep up with the demands of the province as it slowly came back to life again.

There is one episode I want to relate before we get into the second Great War years. By the late fall of 1940 we were beginning to get ahead with our home lives. The house next door was finished mother and father were living there and were very happy, we had managed to save enough money to buy a second hand Ford Model A two door sedan with only two thousand miles on it. It had come in to the valley new and had only made one trip out of the valley hence the low mileage. We got it for two hundred dollars cash and had polished it up and had spent many happy hours with our two boys out on fishing trips and picnics.

As near as I can recall it started on a Thursday in the third week of October 1940. We had heavy snowfalls up in the mountaintops before that and none down in the valley. All day Thursday it poured down and early Friday morning a strong very warm south wind blew.

You could see the snow melting very fast and the mountainsides were covered with streams running down all over. I was standing in the yard with Harold Thorne an old timer who had been through the 1921 flood and he told me that he was going to get home right away as he had to go across the Mamquam River and he didn't want to get stuck on this side of it if we were going to have a flood. This was soon after lunch when we were speaking so he took off.

The rain slacked off somewhat later in the afternoon but this strong warm wind kept on blowing. As we left the shop at quitting time the Mamquam River had flowed over its banks and was just starting to flow over the railway tracks just north of the north yard crossing. There were only one or two houses there at that time and a small farm. We were going back and forth to work in a small motorcar on rail that held about twenty men. We called it Sparky, as it was powered with a gasoline engine that stuck up through the floor. When I got home I told Mary that I though that we were going to have a bad flood and that we had better get downtown right away and stock groceries before the stores closed which lucky for us we did. After supper to be on the safe side I went out in my workshop in the shed and put up all my tools and any thing else that I could think of on top of my workbench. I was nervous all during the evening and I kept going out side and listening to the roar of the water coming down the mountain sides and the sound of the Squamish River as at that time it took a sharp turn and the full force of the river hit the rip rap on the P.G.E. grade just below the crossing of the south end of the yards.

I took my last look outside about midnight the rain had almost stopped and there was no water except the usual rainwater runoff around our house on Wilson Crescent. I then went to bed, as I had to go to the shop in the morning. I was awakened about six thirty in the morning by a sloshing sound around the house, so I leaped out of bed and looked out of the window. My God! There was the dirty brown Squamish River running right by and around our house. I yelled at Mary and the kids to get up right away, pulled on my clothes and my hip waders and went out side, I could walk around all right at that time so I went in to the shed and tried to save the vegetables in the root house but it was too late. The next thing I did was to corral all the wooden sidewalks that I could as they were floating away. I got some on top of the others and made a sort of a raft with nails and rope. Then I tied the raft up to the back porch. I couldn't do any thing about the car, as the water by this time was getting too deep for my waders, it was coming up so fast.

The next thing we did was to get everything in the house up as high as we could. I got blocks of wood from the shed and put up the piano with the help of Mary and the boys then any thing that would be damaged by water we put up on the kitchen chairs and table or took it up stairs. By this time the water was to high for me to go out side in my hip waders and there was quite a heavy current running between our house and mother and dad's place next door.

The next thing to do was to try to get over to the folks place next as their house was lower than ours, I had put a couple of big bean poles on the raft when I tied it up to the

130

back door so Harold and I got on the raft and poled, or I should say let the current take us over to the front of the little house next door. Well! There was mother sitting with her knee rubber boots on dangling in the water in the living room, Dad smoking his pipe with his rubber boots on feet propped up on a chair both taking things very calmly even though there was six inches of water running through the house. They had been up since the crack of dawn getting things as they thought up out of the floodwater danger. Their method was to put all the wooden kitchen furniture on top of the chesterfield and the dressers and like things up on the beds. They were in somewhat of a panic when they were doing this I guess so when they had done what they thought was all they could they sat down and awaited the future.

The water was coming up fast so Harold and I did what we could to save a few things but we had to get them out of the house and over to our place. We got a butter box and put it in the middle of the raft got mother to put on her hat and coat and then came the moment of truth, would the raft hold Harold, Mother and me? I can still see her face as she looked at that frail raft and that fast running muddy water, but she trusted me. She picked up her skirts and gave a big sigh and stepped on the raft and sat down on the box. When Harold and I got on the raft, it just floated with the combined weight of the three of us but when we cast of from the house and started to pole back to our place we had to push pretty hard to pole against the current. Every time we pushed the raft would go under the water about six inches and the water would swirl around mother's feet, finally we got to the steps in the front of our house and mother stepped off the, raft on to our front porch. I think she had held her breath from the time we had cast off until she stepped on our front porch. Then it was back over to the little house for Dad. This trip wasn't as bad as he didn't weigh nearly as much as my mother. Mary made them some breakfast and then we started to get more troubles.

First our front steps that were made of wood floated away with the current, our woodpile that was back of the house took off and disappeared in to the bush behind the house. Then down the road came a man Irwin Thorne in an Indian dugout canoe. He asked me if he could do any thing for me and I said yes. Take me down to my boathouse on the lower end of town by the dyke so I can get my little boat that I used for duck hunting and I can row back up here with it. So he paddled in through our front gate, I got aboard grabbed a paddle and away we went down the middle of Cleveland Avenue until we got to the Squamish Hotel. There I saw a kid rowing around in a small boat which when I got close enough to it I recognized as mine. It was young Dick Dawson. Being in not to good a humor I said, "What in Hell are you doing with my boat?" "Well you weren't using it so I thought I might as well so I bust in to your boat house thinking I might help someone", he replied. I said, "Baloney, you want my boat so you could make a few bucks ferrying people around like you did on the last two floods we had down town."

So with a few more choice remarks I got in to my boat, thanked Irwin for the ride, took the kid home, and rowed all the way from Fourth Street downtown up against the current back to our house. By the time I got home the water was just starting to come in to the house through the front door. We had no wall-to-wall carpet in those days, just linoleum or wood floor with scatter rugs around, however we knew that we were going to have a mess to clean up when the water went down.

I got in to the shed and got a fence and wood bit and bored two or, three holes through the floor in the house. Then with the aid of the boat I was able to get to the outside water tap and couple a garden hose to it and take it into the house. We watched the water come up to the level of the base boards, about six inches then it held at that level for awhile. All at once it started to go down and as it finally got below the floor level we started to work.

Along with the water we had a skim of stove oil going through the house that gave off an offensive smell and stayed in the house for days. However as the water was receding we started washing out the house with the garden hose and brooms. It was a mess; even with all the clean water we poured in to the house with the garden hose it was years before the silt from the flood waiter stopped coming out of the joints in the flooring. Needless to say it was weeks before we got all the mess cleaned up in our house and mother's house and yards. There was no such thing as help from the government in those days. We all had to stand the cost of the losses ourselves and replace our furniture and such when we could afford it. Some people in the company cottages downtown had the water in their homes over top of the piano keys. Others, including us, had to take the engines of our cars apart right away and clean and dry them out.

The whole cause of the flood goes like this. The strong warm winds from the south caused the heavy snow pack up past the thousand-foot level to melt very fast. This caused a fast run off in the Squamish, Elaho, Mamquam, Cheakamus, and Cheekeye Valleys to such an extent that the canyons in the various valleys became blocked with debris. They all then became dams backing up the water in each valley. These dams all let go at approximately the same time causing a very fast rise in the rivers. In the upper Squamish I saw silt left from the flood up the trees as high as I could reach, some of those people were trapped in the attics of their houses for a considerable time. There used to be a large field about half a mile past the house at the end of the pavement up there now. The Squamish with the force of the current rolled up the sod off this field in huge rolls was about four or more feet high. Pushed these rolls up against the bush and devoured the field. It just turned the field in to silt and took it down the river. The Cheekeye River dammed at the canyon just below the highway bridge, this let go and roared down its channel until it hit the Cheakamus River. It hit with such force that it changed the channel pushing tons of rocks in the river bed and pushing the Cheakamus River over to the rock wall that is at that point, as it surged it lifted the road bridge off its foundations took it down river and smashed it to bits.

In the meantime the Mamquam River had taken the road bridge off its foundation floated it down past what was left of the P.G.E. bridge and taken it out to the sea. As this

132

bridge was a Howe truss it was intact and was not damaged to any extent. A further note, this bridge was towed into Darrell Bay kept there for some time and when the road was put through to Britannia it was hauled up the road and was the first bridge over Shannon Creek. As all the water was coming down the rivers we had an exceptionally high tide that backed the water up. As the upper part of the valley became full it poured down into the lower part. The Squamish River broke through the P.G.E. Track at Buckley's Crossing as that part of the grade took the full force of the river at that time. There was no passage straight through as there is now. That was man made later on.

As the water from the rivers poured down into the town from the north so the tidewater broke through the dykes in the lower end of town until the two waters met. The day was quite warm and every so often we would go out on our front porch and say hello to people going past in boats. Owen Reeve who was just a teenager at that time was out on his back porch. His father and mother were in Vancouver so he was all-alone. He was marooned but not in any danger so to make the best of things there he was with a bottle of scotch in one hand and his trumpet in the other blowing his head off with the dance tunes of the day From what I gathered from other people the valley was a complete sheet of water all the way from what is now Garibaldi Estates down to the water front. In our own case all we could see from Wilson Crescent was water in all directions with quite a heavy current running towards the waterfront.

By Saturday we were able to get going on the outside to get things straightened around I left Mary in charge of the boys as they could help her to quite an extent and Harold Bailey and I went up to the shops. What a mess there. The Car shop floor was covered with silt up to four inches thick in places, covering tools and equipment that had been left on the floor at the end of the day shift. In the Paint shop there was a whole coach set of doors and windows that had been freshly painted and varnished and was ready to put on the coach the next week. This then was just a small shop with a closed door.

The water had got in to about a depth of eighteen inches, a five gallon can of black roof paint which had been opened had upset from floating in the water, the black paint had spread all over inside the paint shop and as the water receded it painted everything black including those freshly painted set of doors and windows with a coat of this sticky, wet black paint. There was no doubting the height that the water had been in the shop. Other buildings of the shop complex were in the floodwaters so it was impossible to carry out our regular work coming Monday morning. On top of that there were washouts of the track between the town and the shop that had to be repaired before we had rail communication between the shop and the town. When the men came in on Monday morning they were told that the shops were closed down until the cleanup was finished, as there was no work for them at their regular occupations. However those who wanted to would be put on the section gang payroll and could go to work helping to clean up and repair the tracks. Nearly every one went to work as section men as they knew that the sooner the mess was cleaned up the sooner they would get back to their regular jobs.

In a few days the shops were opened again, it took us a couple of weeks to get things back in place, dried out and the car going again, all that winter we had to eat our stored vegetables from the root house that tasted of a stove oil flavor. Mary and I didn't mind it so much but the boys rebelled to some extent. Years later when they were adults the told me that they used to dread the days when they came home from school and they could see their mother preparing vegetables from the root house. It was years before the silt stopped coming out of the floor when you walked over it, or lifted a rug or linoleum. Some of the older native people said that this was the worst flooding of the valley they had seen and they had seen quite a few.

Before I go on, I want to go back a few years to 1937. Mr. Yarwood the druggist and some other men from Vancouver got interested in a good showing of gold in the Ashloo Valley about eight miles in from the Squamish River. It was put on the stock market and shares were sold to finance the venture. A ferry was built to cross the Squamish just past the end of the pavement large enough to hold a truck so supplies could be brought up from Squamish to the packers cabins about two miles up the river on the opposite side of the river. There the truck was unloaded and all materials including food for the camp at the mine site where carried by pack train up the mountain trail into the mine. Later when the mine was producing, all the gold concentrate was packed out by the pack train and taken to Squamish and then to Vancouver by boat. The pack train was under the direction of Jonny Ryan, an old time packer who is still around Squamish.

The gold vein was very rich; the concentrate was the richest ever produced in any mine up to that time. It had to be to produce enough revenue to keep the mine going. It caused a great deal of interest around the province and further shares were issued. I made my first and last investment in mining stocks. The two certificates cost me seventy-five dollars originally. They had been transferred from one share each that I originally bought, Alas and alack the vein suddenly took an offshoot and disappeared. The company spent all the rest of the funds available trying to find where the damn thing went to but when the money was all gone the mine had to close. My hopes of riches were dashed to the ground.

Writing about the flood brought this back to mind as I described how the flood started with the fast run off. This also happened in the Ashloo Canyon where the mine was located. The water rose so high that after the flood had subsided the owners went back in to see what damage had been done to the mine they found nothing left. The flood had taken every thing away including the concentrator that was fairly high up the bank. The whole thing was wiped out. Later on in the seventies other attempts were made to find the vanished vein but to no success.

However this experience put the thought in to every hunter and fisherman mind that some day he might stumble over another out cropping such as the Ashloo was as he wandered around through the part of the country he was in. This happened to me.

I was hunting with a couple of my friends in the mountains between the Cheakamus and Squamish valleys, the day was cloudy and the terrain was very difficult to hunt in as the small valleys and draws crisscrossed one another so your were continually scrambling up and down these draws. I was making my way through a very thick growth of young firs when I came to a natural basin shaped like a horseshoe, the sides where quite steep, about eighteen feet down to the bottom of the basin. I managed to find a foothold or two and got down to the basin floor. It was a beautiful place, quite damp with a deep carpet of moss covering the whole basin floor. As I rolled a cigarette and looked around me admiring the place the sun broke through the cloud and lit up the place so it could have a setting for a scene from Walt Disney's Seven Dwarfs movie. However there was something wrong. The sun was at my back and I was walking to the south. Also by my watch it was just about noon.

I started to feel a bit of a panic, as I knew that I was completely turned around and lost. Long ago I had lost touch with my companions so it was no use trying to call out for them, however I saw that the basin narrowed down to a small canyon running towards the direction of the sun. I said to myself, "Stathers you are lost, don't panic let's go down that canyon and have the lunch in my bum pack and think this out". That was a very hard thing to do was to make myself turn around and go in the opposite direction than what I had been going. I went down this canyon a few hundred yards and found a big tree that was on a bit of a rise and quite dry so I was able to sit down and have my bite to eat. After I had finished and rolled a cigarette I got to my feet and in doing so I kicked over some rocks that were at the base of the tree, two or three of these rocks were partially white quartz, like the vein that I had seen in the Ashloo Mine so I picked them up. By the Lord Harry, there were those dull yellow flakes embedded in the quartz which I knew were gold. Where did they come from? I looked up the side of the small canyon and saw a smooth rock face, so I climbed up to the face of this bluff and there it was. A vein of white quartz about a foot thick running along the face of this rock for about ten feet then it sloped down and disappeared in to the ground. I was excited of course so I filled up my little pack with the rocks that had come from this vein and started to find my way out.

I climbed up out of the canyon and as it was nearly one o'clock I headed in the direction of the sun. After traveling for about an hour I was on the top of a large knoll and I got a glimpse of a lake which I thought was Evans Lake, sure enough as I got closer to it there it was and I knew were I was so I came out of the bush met my friends and went home. When I got there I took the rocks to Mr. Yarwood who said that he would take them to Vancouver the next time he went and have them assayed. This he did and he told me later that they assayed out as very good samples, but he would have to have more than that to have an estimate made of the worth of the find.

The next thing to do was to go back in there and find the showing, stake a claim, and bring out some more samples. I knew where to start from the valley bottom as we had followed Levitt's trail along the bottom of the hill for about a half a mile past his house which was were the Outdoor School is now. We had then started up the hill for quite a while the three of us together then split up and headed south to come out at the Evans Lake Trail where I eventually got. Lloyd Ingraham and my two boys made two trips in the country that I thought that I had covered when I found the showing but we never found it. That is real rough country up there. So there it is. It may be of no value and again it might be a real rich find. One thing I do know is that I will never know if it is or isn't.

In 1940 the Canadian Government had began to realize the seriousness of the war in Europe and started to organize Canada to its full capacity. One of the first things they did was to have a National Registration of all the adults in the country and the skills that each one had in order to place people in the jobs that might be required to enable the country to put out its maximum effort to play our part in the war. Then all people of German or Italian origin who were not Canadian citizens had to be disarmed and were not allowed to have guns of any description.

My registration certificate and Special Police Identification is in the pouch at the back of the book. As I said before, firearms had to be taken away from any enemy aliens in the district. At that time we had the British Columbia Provincial force controlled by the Province enforcing the laws of the land. The constable in charge of the Squamish Detachment was a well built young man named Pat Fox. We were quite friendly with Pat and his wife Kay. We played bridge with them and often visited back and forth. Pat talked me in to becoming a member of the Special Police so I was given an arm band Identification and took instruction on the law, how to make arrests, and so on. Sometimes he would drive up to the house after supper and say, "Let's go for a ride Eric", so I would hop in the car and take off. Usually he wanted a back up if he was taking a gun away from someone or a witness when making an arrest. After our only doctor died, he would get me when some one was injured and needed First Aid and help to get the patient away to Vancouver.

One night that stands out in my mind was the evening that we took the guns away from Ben Ogle. Now Ben was somewhat of a hermit who lived all alone in a little log shack about fifteen miles north of Squamish up the Cheakamus Valley. He was a German and never been naturalized though he had lived up there for years. He was seldom seen, except by the train crews as he would stand by the train tracks on the way freight days and the crew would throw out a newspaper or old magazines for him. He was very suspicious of people and had at times run people off his place with a shotgun. I knew him to speak to as I used to go by his shack quite often when I was fishing the river. He used to ask me to get him a spawning salmon for his cats so it was easy for me to do, as I would be wearing my waders. We had to hike in quite a way and as we got near his place I asked Pat how were going to get his guns away from him without risking a shot in the rear end. Pat said, "You get him to show you his garden and keep him there while I slip around to the shack and pick up the guns". Well this worked very well, as I was praising on what a good gardener he was Pat got

136

in to the shack and got hold of his rifle and shotgun. Ben went in to a frenzy of rage but he could do little against the both of us, Pat knew that he had to do something for the man as he lived off the fish in the river the game in the woods and, his garden, so he made arrangements for him to go in to the Old Men's Home at Kamloops before the winter set in.

The next thing we had to do as the Japanese were making war like noises and taking sides with the Axis Powers was to organize the Air Raid Precaution shortened to A.R.P. for Squamish. The government supplied all equipment and a warning siren was set up on the top of the P.G.E. Hall. Wardens were set up for the various parts of the town under Mr. Bailey. Extra firemen were trained and all equipment of which we had only two hand pulled fire hose carts but lots of hose. Mr. Alex Munroe looked after this. I had to train and look after the ambulance staff which we trained two teams of four men the ambulances were the two grocery delivery trucks. Dr. Paul set up an emergency hospital with nine beds and nursing staff consisting of what ex-nurses were in the town and the ladies who had taken First Aid. Mary was one of those. Pat Fox was the headman as it was government sponsored and he had direct contact with the center in Vancouver or Victoria. This was organized very quickly and this was the real thing, not a first of July picnic. So the next thing to do was to see how the whole organization would work in the black of night. It was black too as every house or lighted building had to black out their windows and show no lights after dark. On top of that you had to paint out the top half of your car headlights so it would be more difficult to see the lights from the air.

The next thing to do was to test out our readiness to see if the whole unit worked properly. An evening was picked and the sirens set off. Pat Fox had set up some phosphorus flares at various places around the town. He ignited these at different intervals to keep the Firemen busy. I had placed people at other places with different injuries for the ambulances to treat and take to the hospital for the doctor and nurses to treat. The Wardens were on patrol making people black out their houses and also with helpers with their pails of water and stirrup pumps putting out any small fires that started in their area. After it was over we held a meeting of the top brass, picked out the faults but all in all we considered that the town had done very well for the first alarm.

There were some funny incidents that came out of this test, one of them I must tell as we had a good laugh from it later. Charley was a warden and Shorty was his assistant with the stirrup pump and the pail of water. The stirrup pump was a heavy-duty pump like a bicycle pump. You put your foot on the metal part that had a projecting leg on it and the suction part in the pail or any source of water, About twenty feet of hose was attached to the pump with a nozzle on the end that could be adjusted to either spray or send a stream.

They ran up to one of these fires that Pat had set and started on the prescribed procedure. Shorty was on the pump and Charley on the end of the hose at the fire. Nothing happened, no water. Charley is hollering to Shorty to pump, "Pump you So and So"! As the fire gets brighter Charley looks around at Shorty and now by the light of the fire he can see what's the matter. In the blackout and with all the excitement of the night Shorty has put his foot in the pail of water along with the stirrup and is pumping air like mad as the pump part is on the outside of the pail. They got quite a ribbing over that for some time.

All this may seem ludicrous to the reader now to think that a small town like Squamish would be attacked by enemy raiders but, one must stop and think that there were only three routes to take to get from the West coast to the East. Namely the P.G.E. with our main fuel tank right at the shore line and the Cheakamus Bridge over the canyon at 19 mile which could easily be put in to the river with a charge of dynamite. The C.N.R. and the C.P.R. twin bridges in the Fraser Canyon and the old Alexandria Highway Bridge just past Yale. All these routes could have been cut with a few well-placed charges of explosives and cut off all materials moving from east to west or west to east. At that time there were no airplanes large enough to carry any amounts of cargo and train moved most people and materials. Bus travel was very limited from the east on account of the hazardous route through the Fraser Canyon and as gasoline was rationed there wasn't too much for bus transportation. All these activities were at the directives of the Federal Government and they furnished all supplies for the A.R.P.

Guards were placed on these places mentioned and also on the Fraser Bridge at Lillooet and the large wooden trestle at Clinton. Material and people that could get to Clinton via P.G.E. could go by road to either Ashcroft or Kamloops.

Soon after our test, we were advised that a Provincial Test would be made of the A.R.P. at the same time over the whole Province. No warning would be given and the Provincial Police would set off the signal for the sirens to go off. The evening it happened, the sirens went off, everyone hurried to their appointed duties. The town was blacked out and all was in readiness for what was to come. However I was rushed to the home of Dr. Paul. He had been out in his garden when the alarm was given burning some rubbish in the excitement of trying to put out the fire in order to get to the temporary hospital that was his post. He had a heart attack and when I got there he was in the house on the bed. He had oxygen in the house but he was too far-gone for my team and I to revive him.

This left us with no doctor in the town and until we got a doctor to come to town I had to look after the accidents in the area. They came from as far away as Darcy. With the help of a couple of the ambulance crew and sometimes the Provincial Police we could get them patched up and if necessary away to Vancouver on the Union steamship or on the Miss Victoria, a large water taxi based at Porteau. Mrs. McRea looked after the women, and delivered the babies when necessary. She was a trained nurse and was well regarded in the town. My wife had to do her share too, as she had taken First Aid when people came to the house for help if I was away on a wreck she did what she could also. I learned a lot about First Aid in that time as we had all different types of injuries and many a wound I pulled together with adhesive tape, which healed very nicely and left very little scarring. We never accepted money for this work as it against the code of First Aid. When it was offered I would ask the patient to replace the material that we had used to fix him up, but we very rarely got any thing back and if it wasn't for having the use of the material supplied by the A.R.P. we would have been considerably out of pocket.

We went on like this for about eighteen months, then the Medical Association of B.C. sent us an old retired doctor who had been an ear, eye, and throat man serving the Indians up north somewhere. I shall not mention his name for obvious reasons; he will be referred to as Dr. B. He set up shop in an old two-story building long since torn down on Cleveland Avenue opposite where Merv Foote's Men's Wear is today. He used the downstairs part as his home and office. He had a single bed, a couple of chairs, a wood stove, a table, cupboard and a collection of pots and pans and dishes either laying on the table or on the stove or cupboard. Instead of carrying the ashes from the stove outside he used to just rake them out on the floor in front of the stove. Any time I had to go in there there were dirty dishes pots and pans with their sooty bottoms lying on the table or cupboard top. When a patient came in he would move the pots aside and work off the table without wiping the oilcloth that covered the top of the table. Most unsanitary would you say. He would reach in to his bag and come out with a spool of black thread and a needle and proceed to sew up a wound without sterilizing either the needle or thread. Another thing he used to do that he told me about it was to make up a mixture of water and strawberry extract to give to the Indians as a prescription for whatever ailed them.

He was useless in an emergency and when bad cases were brought down by speeder on a stretcher from up the line the police would call on me and a couple of the ambulance crew and we would do what we could to keep the patient going until he could be transported to Vancouver.

Other people at times after seeing him would be very unhappy with what he did or didn't do and would come up to our house for advice or further treatment. This put Mary and I in a very difficult position as we couldn't over ride the decision of the doctor without being liable for prosecution if any thing went wrong with the patient which could be blamed on our treatment. However in a few cases the patient was in such a condition that I did what I could for him. Most of these people came from up the line from logging camps and farmers from Pemberton who had to catch the train back to their home the same day.

I was persuaded by a few of the concerned citizens of the town, one being the pharmacist, to go down to see the head of the medical society in Vancouver. The pharmacist Mr. Yarwood made the appointment and paid my expenses including boat fare and hotel bill for two nights. Well I walked in to the office that was then on Granville Street near the Birks Building. I introduced myself to a portly and important looking man sitting behind a big desk and proceeded to tell him my side of the story. How I was concerned about the health of the town and the responsibilities that I had to take on account of the doctor's method of practice and inability to handle serious accident cases. After I had finished he stood up behind his desk pointed his finger at me and said, "How dare you an ordinary civilian with just First Aid training come in here and ostracize a doctor. What right have you to think that you know more than a member of the medical profession." The tirade continued on and on, I was very embarrassed as my wife and two other men were listening to the calling down I was getting. Finally I lost my cool, interrupted him, and told him in no uncertain terms what I thought of him and that he was lucky that I didn't haul him over the desk and thump some pompous manner out of him. With that off my chest I stormed out of the office and came home.

I guess it did some good though, for a few months after the company doctor from Woodfiber came over twice a week until Doctor Kindree arrived. From then on I left it to him although I did help him on some occasions with serious accidents until we got the hospital built. As my work at he shop was becoming more demanding, I got one of the ambulance crew Mr. Moule to take an Industrial course and after he had obtained his certificate he helped out in the shop First Aid Room and as time went on he took over entirely and I backed away from the First Aid work entirely and let my ticket lapse.

In February of 1942 the Canadian Army established the British Columbia Pacific Coast Militia Rangers. Individual units were recruited in most of the towns, villages, logging, and construction camps from the Yukon border to the southern border. The Squamish Unit was numbered 83 Company. We had about sixty men and boys in our company. They were from many groups; those too old join the services and those too young, most fifteen and sixteen years old. Then those by reason of their jobs were judged to be of more value to the war effort to keep on producing at home than to be in the services. We also had some of the local Indians in our group. As the wages in the shipyards and logging camp were a lot higher than the wages paid by the Railway, we lost many of our mechanics as they left for more money. However the War Department let us keep our apprentices so most of them were in our unit also. Most of the men and boys were fishermen and went out hunting so they knew how to take care of themselves in the woods and were good shots.

After we had our Provincial Test of the A.R.P. and it was all organized I was asked to join the Rangers by the Captain, Mr. Smith Frost the Forestry Warden. This I did and had to take the same oath as the regular Army to serve King and Country with the rider that we wouldn't be used if necessary any were else than in B.C. I was given the rank of Sargent and told to look after the First Aid training of the unit. Later on I was given other duties to perform and finally at the end of the war I held the rank of First Lieutenant and second in command of the unit.

Squamish Pacific Coast Militia Rangers Company 83 1945
– Front row second from left T. Clarke, S. Frost, E. Stathers, A. Thorne, D. Kirkwood, E. Aldridge.
Third row middle behind Eric Stathers is his son Harold Stathers.

Our equipment was a dry back khaki woods jacket and pants, dry back loggers hat, badges, and insignia. We were issued Winchester 30-30 carbines and fifty rounds of ammunition. We had to have a supply of dried food and chocolate enough to last a week at home. Unlike many Militia units of the past we took our arms and ammunition home, only the machine guns, grenades, and flares were kept at the Captain's house.

Our headquarters were in the P.G.E. hall that is now the Hudson House on Second Avenue. An emergency meeting place was the small caves that are in the rocks under the B.C. Electric right of way up in Bughouse Heights. Captain Frost was in the First World War so he was familiar with Army drill and he soon whipped the unit into some sort of order drilling us in the hall during the first winter. In the field we were broken up into commando groups of nine men under a Corporal. This was a squad. Then two squads were under the command of a Sargent. A company Sargent Major took over the drill of the whole unit until in field exercises the unit was under the command of the Captain with duties delegated to either the first or second lieutenant.

In addition nearly every week we had different officers from the Pacific Command come up from Vancouver to give us training in the various methods of warfare, with emphasis on containing the Japanese and harassing them until the Army could get on the scene. We built a rifle range; a shelter shack, trenches, and crouch shelter were men would be protected when we were throwing grenades.

141

We also put in a trail with movable targets. These were made of plywood and had Jap faces on them to simulate going through an ambush site, the men had to walk this trail spot as many targets as they could and knock them down with a bullet from their rifle. Then an officer would walk through the trail, count the number knocked down, and score the individual on his performance

We held many other field exercises, many in the night time coordinating attacks by different directors, using whatever was at hand to hide faces and camouflage body. Our signalers had direct contact with Woodfiber and Britannia, An arrangement was made with Woodfiber group that a flare wood be sent up from a point on the road near the ferry terminal which was as far as the road went in those days. Some one would see it and tell one of their groups. Then by a special pen like flashlight inside the shell chamber, the light, or the rifle would be aimed at a predetermined point on their shore and the dots and dashes could be seen without been visible from any other point. Britannia could be reached by phone or trail along the route that the road takes now.

One of our Instructors, a Sargent Major Gardiner, was a real tough character. He was from a British Commando unit and said he was a survivor of the Dieppe Raid. You jumped when he barked out commands and lord help those who horsed around when he was giving instructions. One Sunday afternoon at the rifle range we were been taught the use of hand grenades the whole group had to go through this experience. He made us stand in the trench with our heads and shoulders exposed, then he would throw a seven second grenade that is one that would explode in seven seconds from the time that the pin was pulled about fifty feet in front of us. He was timing the explosion time and you had to stand there looking at that grenade until he she shouted down. The next second the grenade would go off and a shower of dirt and branches and leaves would come down on your head. A rather nerve racking experience, but that was one of his ways of teaching discipline because woe to the man who ducked before his command.

There were Ranger units organized on the fish boats as well. They had direct radio link with Pacific Command. U-boats sightings were seen by these boats and after the shelling of a lighthouse and other small incidents they were very alert and reported sightings that never got in to the press. These sighting were kept under wraps so as to not alarm the public. In my opinion the sub or subs that were doing this was to try and get the public alarmed to such an extent that more regular army units would be held at the coast to draw them away from the war zone. But after the Japs landed on the Aleutians we were put on a twenty minute alert for a period of time as they expected a surface attack further down the coast to draw the American Army units away from the invasion in Alaska.

As near as I can recall in early 1944 we started to get the Jap balloons coming over the B.C. Coast. I was sent to the Seaforth Barracks in Vancouver to take a two-day instruction course in how to recognize these balloons and instruct the group on how to handle them if one came down in our area. So with some authority I can describe these weapons. The Japanese Government started a program among the villages and towns to produce these balloons as a help to their war effort. On the day that each balloon was launched from their particular village, a holiday was proclaimed.

The balloon bags were made of several layers of some kind of paper glued with a flexible kind of varnish, as the specimen that I saw was quite stiff and very flammable. It was pear shaped and attached to a round basket that had a woven ring around the top portion that the ropes from the balloon were attached to. The ring had a number of mechanical actuated hooks on the outside of the basket. These hooks were to hold either sand bags or incendiary or explosive bombs. Inside the basket was a six-volt battery to open or close the valve that controlled the overhead envelope. These were not hot air balloons as are in common use today. There was also a mechanism that could release the hooks and drop either the sand bags or bombs when directed. The brain of the balloon was an anerode or altimeter that directed the valve to be opened or closed or the release of the hooks.

Now as the prevailing winds are from west to east the balloons were set adrift, and started on their journey that would have taken from three to five days depending on the force of the winds they encountered. During the nighttime as the temperature dropped, as they were over the ocean the first few days they would drop one or two of the sand bags. As the balloon was coming down, due to the decrease in pressure of the gas caused by the cooling temperature. During the day as the heat in the balloon increased the pressure of the gas and it's lifting ability the balloon would rise, if the pressure got too great in the bag the balloon would burst. Again the aneroid would go to work as it did during the night when it actuated the hooks to drop the sand bags, only this time the mechanism it controlled would open the valve that would release some of the gas from the bag to keep the balloon at a predetermined height.

By the time the balloon reached the Canadian or American shores the sand bags had all been dropped. Now the incendiary bombs were dropped to control the height in hope of setting fire to our forests or buildings. When the balloon hit a mountainside or ran out of gas, the balloon would self-destruct and the flammable bag would create a large fire. Some of the balloons carried instead of incendiary bombs, carried a larger single bomb that when the balloon came down the bomb would explode damaging either people or buildings that were in range of the blast. Some of these explosive bombs were duds and from them the Army was able to get the whole balloon for information.

One of these landed in the state of Washington, A minister and his wife and two girls were on a picnic in the woods and came across one of these duds, while they were looking at it and wondering what it was, they picked it up and it went off killing the whole family. These balloons landed all the way from Alaska to the north coast of California and as far inland as Alberta. However, most of them crashed either on the mountains on the west coast of Vancouver Island or on the Coast Range. One was sighted from Squamish going past Garibaldi on a sunny afternoon and the other landed on the hillside near Birken Lake during

143

a rainstorm as the fire started during the rain and there was no lighting reported. To my knowledge no great damage was done by these balloons except for a few fires started and the fatality that I mentioned, however it is an episode of the war that was a worry to some extent.

I served with the Rangers from July 1943 until stand down in October in 1945. We all served voluntarily and without any pay for two and a half years. After stand down we were allowed to keep the rifle we were issued, and our uniform. The ammunition had to be turned in, as it was not suitable for hunting purposes, being steel jacketed. Our parades were held once week and in the weekends were the outdoor maneuvers, so the men of the Rangers donated many thousands of hours toward the defense of the coast.

How we would have conducted ourselves if the Japs had attacked is a moot question, but I think that most of the men were hardy enough to put up some resistance and would have been of great help to the Army as guide when they arrived on the scene. One example of this that was reported to us was an exercise put on by the Army and the Ranger command. Two partial regiments of Army personnel were taken by the Navy to the west coast of Vancouver Island, they were put ashore by landing craft and had to flush out three companies of Rangers who were simulating a Japanese sneak attack. These three companies were from logging camps along the coast and were bush wise and hardy men.

By eleven o'clock the exercise had to be terminated as the Rangers had captured the Army headquarters command post and cut all the communications between them and the rest of the troops. There were more than ten thousand men under arms along the coast and the Japs knew this as the Army made sure that the Japanese command knew what to expect if they had any idea of an attack. According to the reports we got, this had a deterrent effect on them landing on the west coast.

Now the question of reparations for the Japanese who were sent to the Interior of B.C. has come up before the legislature in Ottawa. No doubt there were many instances of deals made by B.C. residents that were very unfair to the Japanese who had to give up their home or fish boats to go to these places that were reserved for them. But they never went hungry and always had shelter. When you read of the atrocities that were inflicted by the Japanese army on our civilians in Singapore and other parts of the east, the death marches that our troops had to endure and the callousness of the way they treated our women and children, the Japanese in B.C. in comparison were very fortunate.

6. EPILOGUE

Eric's memoirs, *My Story* and *In the Ditch,* cover the time period up to 1965 when he retired from the Pacific Great Eastern Railway at age 58 after several heart attacks. Eric and Mary lived a remarkable life during their retirement. They sold their Wilson Crescent home in Squamish and moved to Lillooet, British Columbia, where they lived for about 5 years with Eric's son Harold Stathers and family during the winter in a suite in their home and spent summers at their second home at Gun Lake.

Eric and Mary returned to Squamish around 1970 and lived in an apartment building on Wilson Crescent until purchasing their own home on Britannia Avenue. Here they were in the same community as both sons and all of their grandchildren. Eric helped out in the Irly Bird Lumber Store owned by his sons and continued to be active in the community with his Dixieland band *The Grandma's and Grandpa's* that played for senior's dances. Mary continued to be active in the various community organizations including the hospital auxiliary and Royal Purple. During the winter when health permitted they lived in Tucson, Arizona and travelled to Maui. Summers included trips to Gun Lake until they sold the cabin. Eric Prince Stathers died in April 1986 at the age of 79 years old. Mary continued to live in the family home until her death in November 1992 when she was 85 years.

Nana Mae fly-fishing with Beezer on the dock at Gun Lake.

APPENDIX

Eric Prince Stathers Family Tree drawn by Eric.

Mary Stathers Family tree

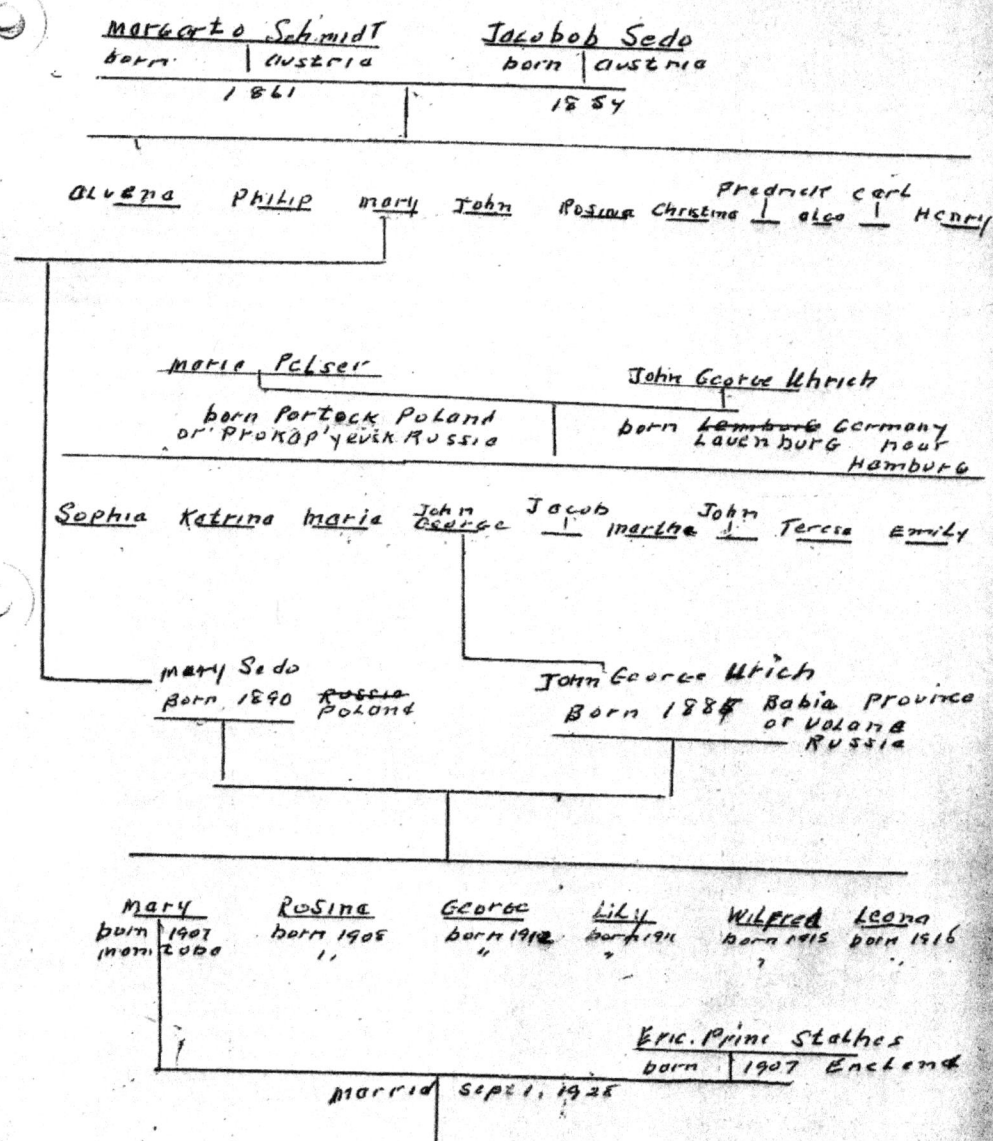

Margarto Schmidt — born Austria 1861

Jacobob Sedo — born Austria 1854

Alvena Philip Mary John Rosina Christina Fredrick Carl Also Henry

Marie Pelser — born Porteck Poland or Prokop'yevsk Russia

John George Uhrich — born Lemburg Germany near Lavenburg near Hamburg

Sophia Katrina Marie John George Jacob Martha John Teresa Emily

Mary Sedo — Born 1890 Russia Poland

John George Urich — Born 1884 Babia Province or Volana Russia

Mary — born 1907 mom Lobo

Rosina — born 1908

George — born 1912

Lily — born 1911

Wilfred — born 1915

Leona — born 1916

Eric. Prine Stathes — born 1907 England

Married Sept 1, 1925

Mary Stathers family tree drawn by Eric.

148

Mary, Harold, Eric, and Jack Stathers, circa 1937.

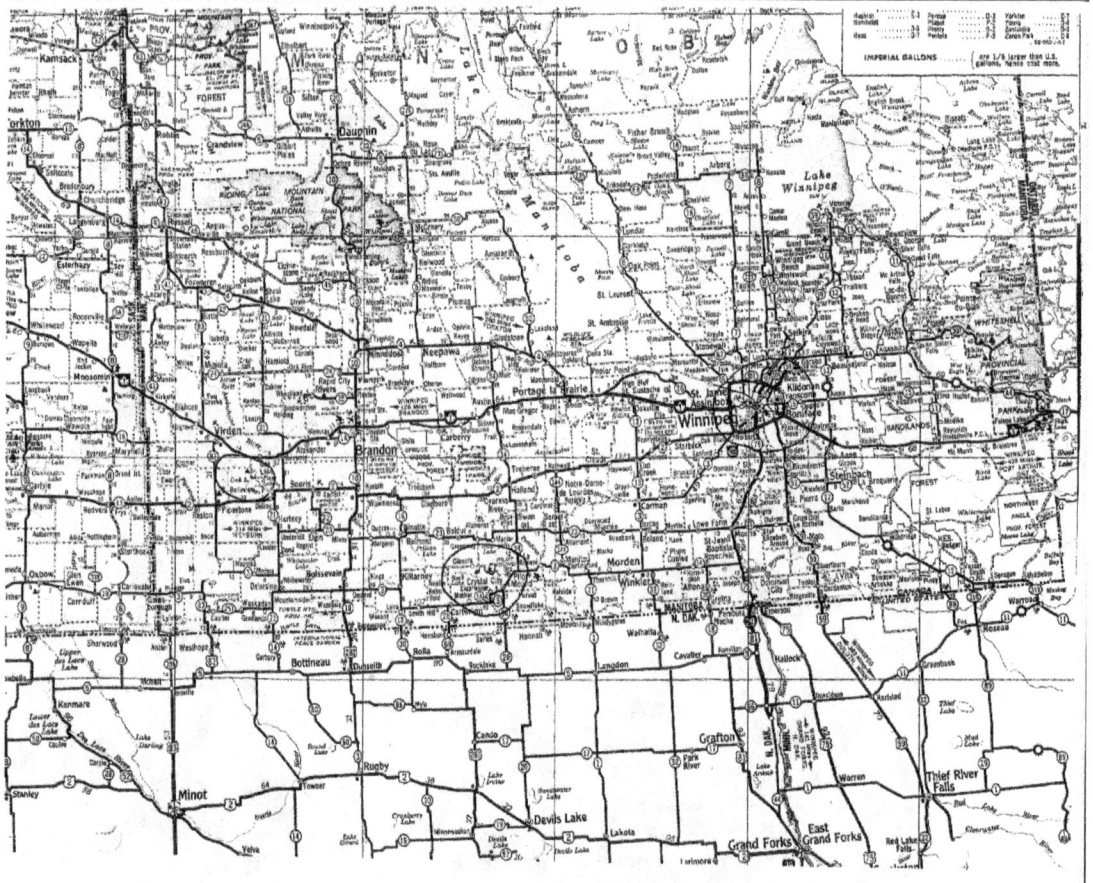

Map with hand-drawn circles by Eric showing the location of the Clearwater farms in relation to Winnipeg. Note the proximity of Clearwater to the North Dakota border.

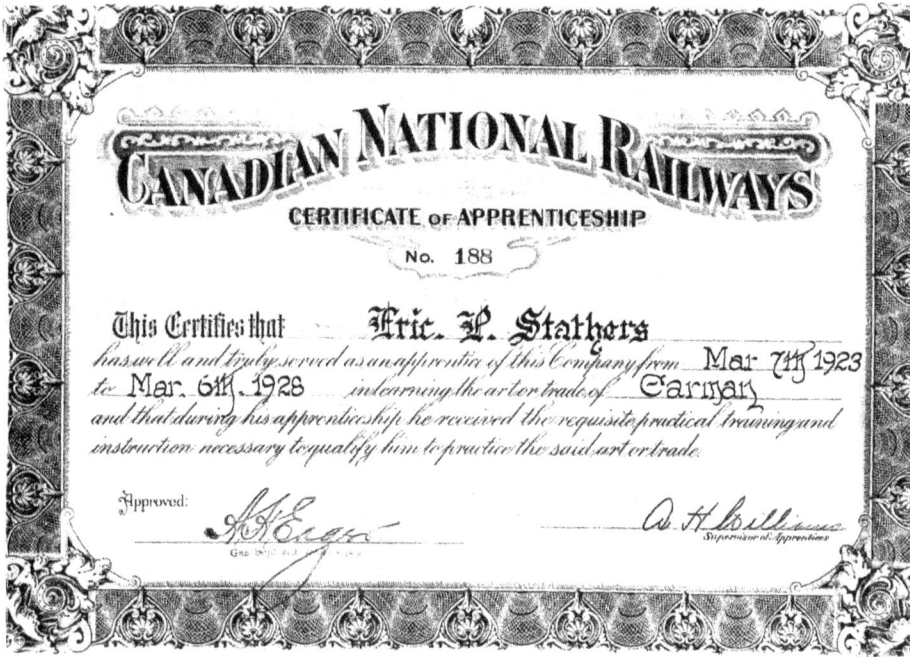

Eric Stather's C.N.R. Certificate of Apprenticeship, 1928.

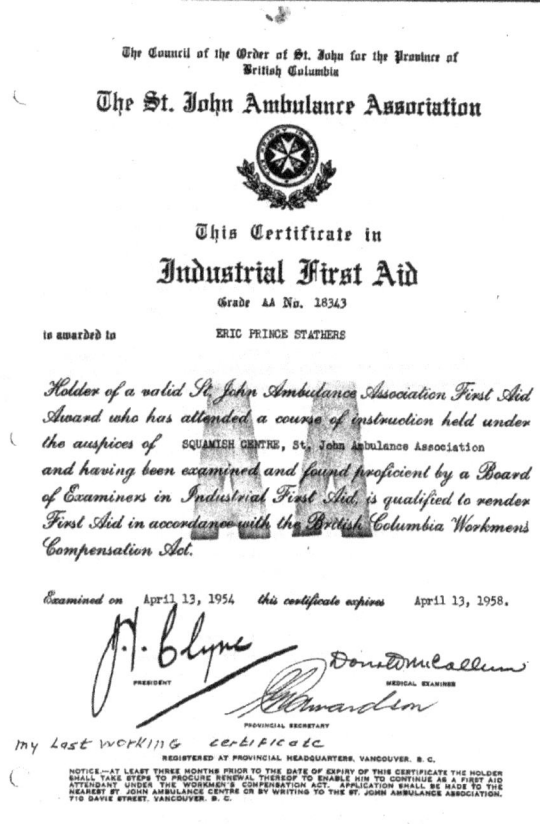

Eric Prince Stathers Industrial First Aid Certificate 1954.

BOOKS BY

ERIC PRINCE STATHERS

IN THE DITCH

Stories of the Pacific Great Eastern Railway, 1929-65

"Eric Stathers knew the Pacific Great Eastern Railway all too well. In the 1920s and 30s, the PGE was a struggling, backwoods railway if ever there was one, and it presented endless challenges to those whose job it was to it running. Eric was Wrecking Foreman at the railway's Squamish shops and he was often called out with his crew to recover wrecked locomotives, cars and equipment all along the tough and mountainous line between Squamish and Prince George, British Columbia. Heavy rain, snow, rockslides, collapsed bridges, washouts and floods were all too frequent occurrences. Not only that, but the railway had a makeshift collection of equipment that took constant attention to keep rolling. This is a fascinating first hand account of a rugged railway and the rugged, tough men who made it survive in the years of the Great Depression and World War II. This book takes you right to trackside to witness the challenges, frustrations, and dangers of working on the Pacific Great Eastern Railway when its survival was problematic, but its role so vital to all those who depended upon it."

Robert D. Turner
Curator Emeritus, Royal BC Museum